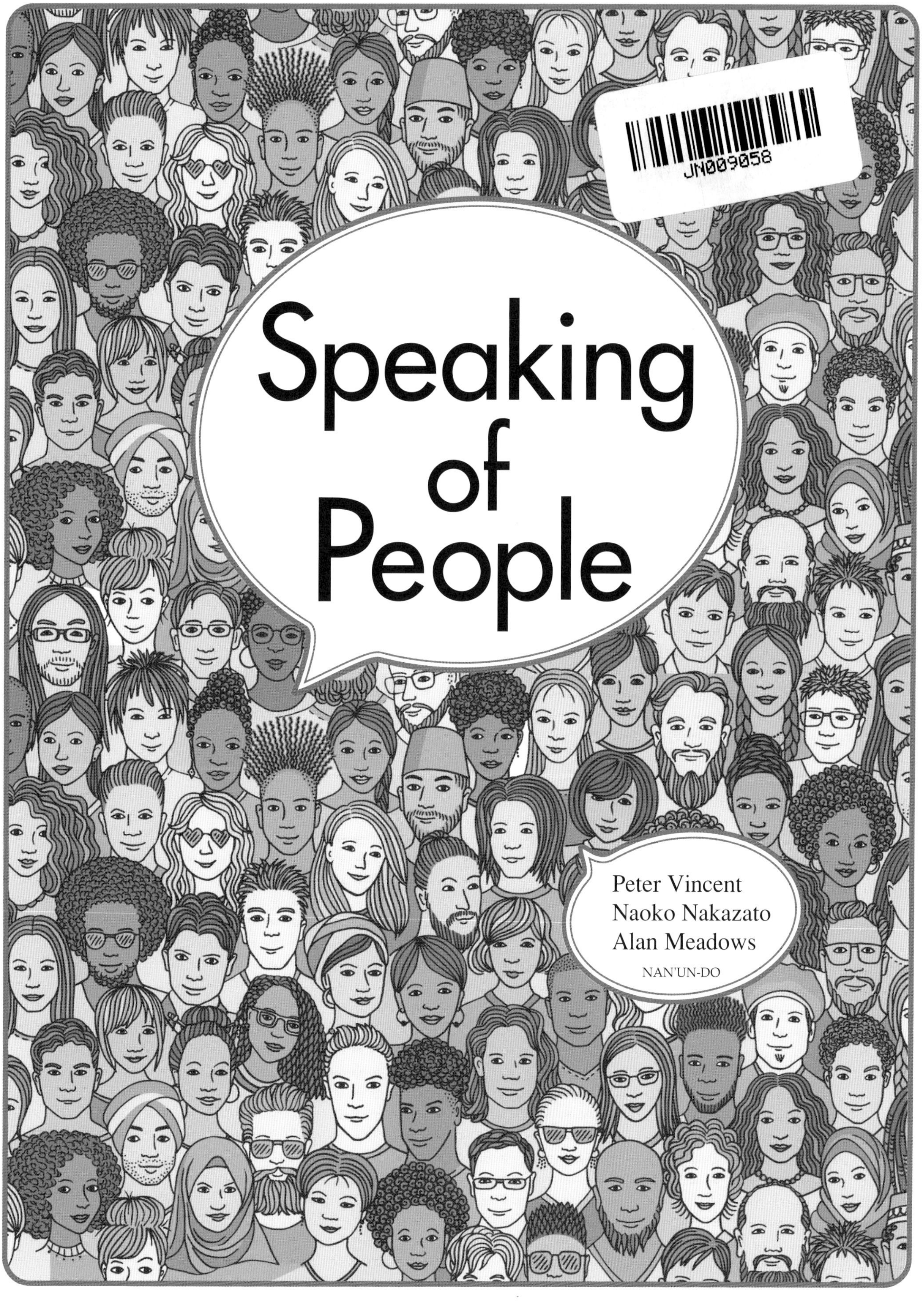

Speaking of People

Peter Vincent
Naoko Nakazato
Alan Meadows

NAN'UN-DO

Download Audio

音声ファイル
無料 DL
のご案内

このテキストの音声を無料で視聴（ストリーミング）・ダウンロードできます。自習用音声としてご活用ください。
以下のサイトにアクセスしてテキスト番号で検索してください。

https://nanun-do.com　テキスト番号［**512053**］

※ 無線 LAN（WiFi）に接続してのご利用を推奨いたします。

※ 音声ダウンロードは Zip ファイルでの提供になります。
お使いの機器によっては別途ソフトウェア（アプリケーション）の導入が必要となります。

※ Speaking of People 音声ダウンロードページは以下の QR コードからもご利用になれます。

Speaking of People

人とつながる英語コミュニケーション

Image Credits:

Front Cover: ©Shutterstock.com

Book: All images ©Shutterstock.com, except:
p. 52 ©Xeravines / Shutterstock.com
p. 56 Practice 3-3 ©zepkatana / Shutterstock.com
p. 134 Practice 10 ©cjmacer / Shutterstock.com

Preface

Welcome to *Speaking of People*, a textbook written for Japanese students of English who are interested in talking about people. The text is designed for active communication with many fun tasks and exercises. It contains various speaking, listening, reading, and writing activities, all with colorful illustrations to help you understand and communicate about people. The textbook includes practice in such things as describing physical appearance, personality, feelings, and experiences.

In order to make the most of this textbook, we would like you to remember one thing: Don't be afraid of making mistakes. Making mistakes and learning from them is how you improve your English skills, so please try your best.

We very much enjoyed writing this textbook and hope that you have an equally enjoyable time speaking about people in English.

Speaking of Peopleにようこそ。本書は人について話すことに興味のある日本人学生のために書かれました。このテキストは活発なコミュニケーションを目的とした多様なアクティビティとロールプレイが盛り込まれています。スピーキング、リスニング、ライティングタスクなどをカラフルなイラストで表現し、人に関する様々なコミュニケーションに役立つアクティビティにしました。その中には、身体的な特徴、性格、感情や経験などを表す練習が含まれています。本書を最も有効に活用していただくために一つ覚えておいてほしいことがあります。間違いを恐れないでください。間違いから学ぶことが英語のスキルを上達させることにつながります。恥ずかしがらず、思い切ってトライしてください。

著者一同にとって、本書を書くことは非常に楽しいプロセスでした。みなさんも、本書を使って人に関する様々な話題を英語で楽しめるようになってほしいと思います。

Peter Vincent（Seitoku University）
Naoko Nakazato（Seitoku University）
Alan Meadows（Seitoku University）

CONTENTS

Speaking of People

by Peter Vincent, Naoko Nakazato, Alan Meadows

Unit 1

Speaking About Yourself

自分について話そう

Speaking

Practice the following dialogues with a partner. After you have practiced the model conversation a few times, substitute the underlined information with the words in the boxes.

以下の会話をパートナーと練習してください。数回練習したら、下線の部分を枠内の表現に言いかえて再度練習しましょう。

Study Tip: Don't just read the dialogues. Try to maintain eye contact with your partner while speaking.

キーポイント：ただ会話を読むだけでなく、パートナーの顔をきちんと見て話しましょう。

Dialogue 1 2

Ken: My name's Ken. It's nice to meet you.(1)

Amber: I'm Amber. Nice to meet you,(1) too.
Are you a psychology* student?

Ken: Yes, I am. I'm a senior.*(2) How about you?

Amber: I study social welfare.* I'm a junior.*

1. Pleased to meet you Good to meet you	2. freshman* sophomore*

Dialogue 2 3

Amber: Are you Japanese?

Ken: Yes, I am. I'm from Tokyo.

Amber: Oh, really? What do you want to do after graduation*?

Ken: I'd like to get a job in psychology. I want to be a counselor. How about you? What do you want to do in the future?

Amber: I want to work in a retirement home.*(1)

Ken: Oh, really?

1. work in a day-care center* help disabled children*

Dialogue 3 4

Ken: Do you have many classes?

Amber: This semester*, I have 15 classes a week. And you?

Ken: Just eight, but I have a lot of homework.

Amber: Do you have a part-time job?

Ken: Yes, I work in a convenience store*(1).

Amber: Oh, yeah? So do I*!

1. work in a restaurant
   tutor* children

* psychology 心理学　senior 大学 4 年生　social welfare 社会福祉　junior 大学 3 年生
freshman 大学 1 年生　sophomore 大学 2 年生　graduation 卒業　retirement home 老人ホーム
day-care center 保育園　disabled children 障害のある子どもたち　semester 学期
convenience store コンビニ　So do I. 私も〜です。　tutor 個人授業をする (家庭教師をする)

Grammar 1 5

Yes/No questions with "be" and "do"

be 動詞と一般動詞 do/does を使った Yes/No 質問文

Are you a graduate* student?	Yes, I am.
Is he a freshman?	No, he isn't. He's a junior.
Do you study sociology*?	No, I don't.
Do they live in Tokyo?	Yes, they do.
Does she like Tokyo?	Yes, she does. She thinks it's an exciting city.
Do you want to be a teacher?	Yes, I do. I want to work in an elementary school*.
Are you busy now?	Yes, I am.
Do they have a lot of homework?	Yes, they do.

* graduate student 大学院生　sociology 社会学　elementary school 小学校

▶Practice 1 Matching 質問に合った答えをさがそう

Put the correct letters for the answers in the spaces.

1～8までの質問に対する最も適切な答えをAからHの中から選びましょう。

______	1. Are you a junior?	A.	No, I don't. I study psychology.
______	2. Do you study social welfare?	B.	Yes, I am. I'm a freshman in that department*.
______	3. Are your classes difficult?	C.	Maybe, but I'm not sure* yet.
______	4. Are you a social welfare student?	D.	Yes, I am. I have 16 classes a week.
______	5. Do you live in Tokyo?	E.	Yes, they are. We have a lot of homework.
______	6. Are you busy these days*?	F.	No, I don't. I live in Chiba Prefecture*.
______	7. Do you like studying math*?	G.	No, I'm not. I'm a senior.
______	8. Do you want to work in a retirement home?	H.	Well, I'm not so good with* numbers, so it's kind of* difficult.

* department 学部、学科　I'm not sure. 確かではない。　these days 最近　prefecture 県
math 数学、算数　be good with ～ ～が得意　kind of 何だか、ちょっと

Grammar 2

Questions with "What," "How," and "Where"

What, How, Where を使った質問

What's your name?	(My name is) Megan Williams.
What do you study?	(I study) Economics*.
What do you do?	I'm a university student. I study international relations.*
What university do you go to?	(I go to) City University.
What do you do in your free time?	(I) Read and play tennis.
What do you want to do in the future?	I want to be a high school counselor.
How old are you?	(I'm) 19 years old.
How do you come to school?	(I come) By train. I take the Chuo Line.
How many people are there in your family?	(There are) Three. I'm an only child*.
How many brothers and sisters do you have?	(I have) One brother and two sisters.
Where do you live?	(I live in) Shibuya.
Where were you born?	(I was born in) Osaka.

* economics 経済学　international relations 国際関係　only child 一人っ子

▶Practice 2 Questions and Answers 自分のことについて答えよう

Write answers that are true for you. Try to add extra information if possible.

自分のことについて答え、追加の情報も加えましょう。

1. What do you do? ______________________________

____

2. What school/university do you go to? ______________________________

____

3. Where do you live? ______________________________

____

4. What do you do in your free time? ______________________________

____

5. How many people are there in your family? ______________________________

____

6. What do you want to do in the future? ______________________________

____

▶Practice 3 Pair Work ペアワーク

Ask your partner questions to obtain the information listed below.

パートナーから以下の情報を聞いて、枠内に書きましょう。

Name: ______________________________

Age: ______________________________

What/do: ______________________________

School: ______________________________

Where/live: ______________________________

Family: ______________________________

Number of brothers/sisters: ______________________________

Free time: ______________________________

Future goal*: ______________________________

* future goal 将来の目標

▶Practice 4 Listening: Introductions 友達を紹介する 7

Listen to the following introduction and write in the missing words below.

英文を聞いて空欄を埋めましょう。

Hello, everybody. I would ______________________________ Ayaka Kobayashi. She's ______________________________ and ______________________________. She lives in Tama Plaza, which is a ______________________________. There are five people ______________________________, her father, mother, sister, brother, and Ayaka. She likes to __________________ TV and ______________________ in her ___________________________. She wants to ______________________________ in the future. She ______________________, so I think she'll be a good counselor. Thank you.

▶Practice 5 Mini-Presentation: Introductions ミニプレゼンテーション

Introduce your partner using the information you wrote down in **Practice 3**. You can also use some of the sentences in **Practice 4** as models.

Practice 3 で得た情報をもとに、パートナーを紹介しましょう。Practice 4 で学んだ表現も使ってみましょう。

▶Practice 6 Find Someone Who ... こんな人を探そう

First, complete the questions on the left of the chart below. Then find someone who answers "yes" to the questions and write their names on the right. Try to talk to as many people as you can.

表の左側の質問文を完成させ、その質問に Yes（否定の質問で聞かれたら答えは No）と答えられる人を見つけたら、右側の欄に記入してください。できるだけ多くの人に質問しましょう。

Example: Question: Do you want to work helping people?
Answer: Yes, I do. (Write down the person's name)

Find Someone Who ...	Name
1. ... wants to work helping people. Question: ______________________________ ?	
2. ... likes to play computer games. Question: ______________________________ ?	
3. ... is interested in psychology. Question: ______________________________ ?	
4. ... is good at math. Question: ______________________________ ?	
5. ... wants to work overseas* in the future. Question: ______________________________ ?	
6. ... likes to play sports. Question: ______________________________ ?	
7. ... has a part-time job. Question: ______________________________ ?	
8. ... has a pet. Question: ______________________________ ?	

* overseas 海外

▶Practice 7 Listening リスニング 8

Listen to two conversations. Which conversation do you think is more successful? Why?

この会話では、誰が上手に会話をしていますか？　なぜそう思いますか？

▶Practice 8 Group Work: Small Talk グループワーク：雑談

When you meet friends or strangers, you often have small talk, a conversation about personal and simple, daily topics. In groups, decide what topics are good for small talk.

雑談や世間話など軽い会話をするときの留意点は何ですか？また、どんなトピックが適切ですか？グループ内で話し合ってみましょう。

Good Topics for Small Talk: 楽しい雑談にするためのトピック選び

1. ________________	5. ________________
2. ________________	6. ________________
3. ________________	7. ________________
4. ________________	8. ________________

▶Practice 9 Pair Work: Small Talk ペアワーク：雑談

Student A: Imagine you are a Japanese who sits next to a foreigner on a flight to Tokyo from overseas. **Student B**: You are the foreigner. Introduce yourselves and talk. Write a dialogue and act it out in front of the class.

国際線の飛行機で隣に外国人が座りました。自己紹介をして、会話を始めます。その際の会話を作ってクラスで発表しましょう。Student A は日本人、Student B は外国人として会話を始めましょう。

Unit 2

What Do You Do?

お仕事は何ですか？

Speaking

Practice the following dialogues with a partner. After you have practiced the model conversation a few times, substitute the underlined information with the words in the boxes.

以下の会話をパートナーと練習してください。数回練習したら，下線の部分を枠内の表現に言いかえて再度練習しましょう。

Dialogue 1 9

Nina: What do you do, Doug?

Doug: I'm a teacher.(1)

Nina: Oh, really? Where do you work?

Doug: I teach at an elementary school.*(2)

Nina: Do you like your job?

Doug: Yes, I do. I like it a lot.

1. counselor social worker*	2. work at a university work for a charity* downtown*

Dialogue 2 10

Martin: Do you have a part-time job, Karen?

Karen: Yes, I work at an Italian restaurant.(1)

Martin: Oh, so you're a server?*(2)

Karen: Yes, that's right.

Martin: So where do you work?

Karen: At a small restaurant near my house.(3)

1. a cram school* a sports club	2. tutor fitness instructor	3. a cram school near the station Tip Top Gym

* elementary school 小学校　social worker ソーシャルワーカー　charity 慈善団体
downtown 街の中心街　server ウエイター / ウエイトレス　cram school 塾

▶Practice 1 Vocabulary 単語表現

Choose the correct word from the box for each picture. Add "s" for plurals.

絵の職業を表す最も適切な単語を枠内から選びましょう。複数形には "s" を忘れずに。

Example:

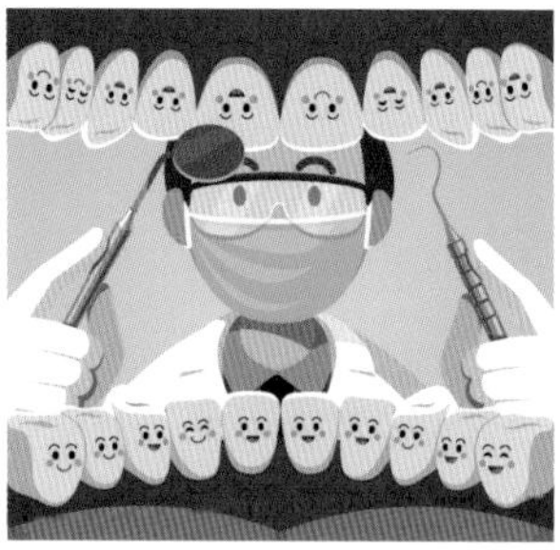

dentist

chef doctor fitness instructor
caregiver* carpenter* server
police officer pilot cashier*
reporter nurse computer engineer

* caregiver 介護者 carpenter 大工 cashier レジ係

1. ______________

2. ______________

3. ______________

4. ______________

5. ______________

6. ______________

7. ______________

8. ______________

9. ______________

10. ______________

11. ______________

12. ______________

Grammar 1

11

Present Simple Tense (with "Wh" questions and answers)
一般動詞現在形（"Wh" 質問と答え）

What **do** you **do**?	I'**m** a student. I ***have*** a part-time job, too.
Where **do** you **work**?	I ***work*** at Super Burger. / I ***work*** in New York.
What **does** he **do**?	He'**s** a caregiver*. He ***works*** in a retirement home*.
What **does** she **do**?	She'**s** a high school teacher. / She ***teaches*** in a high school.
What hours **do** you **work**?	I ***work*** from nine to five.
What days **does** she **work**?	She ***works*** from Monday to Friday.
What days **does** he **get off**?	He ***gets*** off weekends (Saturday and Sunday).

* caregiver 介護士　retirement home 老人ホーム

▶Practice 2 Matching 空欄を埋めよう

Put the correct letter in each space to make a sentence.

1～12 の空欄に入るものを、A～I の中から選びましょう。

_____ 1. A pilot	A. prepares* food.
_____ 2. A police officer	B. works with numbers and money.
_____ 3. A mailman*	C. writes news stories.
_____ 4. A carpenter*	D. serves food in a restaurant.
_____ 5. A nurse*	E. flies* planes.
_____ 6. A chef	F. builds* houses.
_____ 7. A server	G. designs and makes things.
_____ 8. A receptionist*	H. stops crimes*.
_____ 9. A barber*	I. helps sick people.
_____ 10. A reporter	J. greets* clients* and answers telephone calls.
_____ 11. An accountant*	K. cuts hair.
_____ 12. An engineer	L. delivers* letters.

* prepare 準備する　mailman 郵便配達人　carpenter 大工　nurse 看護師　fly 飛行機を操縦する
build 建てる　receptionist 受付け係　crime 犯罪　barber 床屋　greet あいさつする
client 顧客　accountant 会計士　deliver 配達する

▶Practice 3 Listening: What Does She Do? リスニング：彼女の仕事は？

Key Words 12

sales clerk 店員　actor　dentist 歯医者　nurse　baker パン、ケーキ職人　pilot
musician　firefighter 消防士　tour guide ツアーガイド　teacher　computer engineer
patient 患者　medicine 薬　overseas 海外　musical instruments 楽器　pastries パン菓子
department store デパート　clothes 服　passenger 乗客　act 演じる　famous 有名な
selfies 自撮り写真　put out 消す　get out of ～ ～から出る　burning 燃えている
dangerous 危険な　applications アプリケーション、アップ　develop 開発する　teeth 歯

Listen and guess what job the speaker does. Choose the job from the box and write a sentence like the example below. 13
英文を聞いてその人の職業を枠内から選び、例を参考にして文を書きましょう。

Example: You hear: "I work in a large hospital. I take care of* patients* and give them medicine*."
You write: She is (She's) a nurse.

1. ______________________.　6. ______________________.

2. ______________________.　7. ______________________.

3. ______________________.　8. ______________________.

4. ______________________.　9. ______________________.

5. ______________________.　10. ______________________.

* take care of 世話をする　patient 患者　medicine 薬

▶Practice 4 Group Work: Gesture Game グループワーク：ジェスチャーゲーム

You will get a job name. Act out the job without speaking and try to get your group to guess what your job is.
与えられた職業を、口頭ではなくジェスチャーで説明し、グループのメンバーに当ててもらいましょう。

Example: A: Are you a computer engineer?
B: No, I'm not.

▶Practice 5 Pair Work ペアワーク

Look back at the pictures in **Practice 1**. Answer the following questions with a partner. Use your imagination.

Practice 1 に戻り、絵を見てパートナーと以下の質問に答えましょう。想像力を使ってください。

Picture 1. Do they wear hats?
Picture 2. Does she travel?
Picture 3. Does he work outside?
Picture 4. Do they work in a hospital or a clinic?
Picture 5. Does he help people?
Picture 6. Does he work at a desk?
Picture 7. Does she work in a hospital?
Picture 8. Is their job dangerous?
Picture 9. Does he work at home?
Picture 10. Is her job exciting?
Picture 11. Does he work in a store or a restaurant?
Picture 12. Does he build something?

▶Practice 6 Group Work: What's My Job? グループワーク：私の職業は何でしょう？

One person in your group will think of a job. The other members ask questions to try to find out what the job is. The questions should all be "Yes/No" questions. The answers are "Yes", "No" or "Sometimes".

グループ内の一人が職業を一つ選びます。他のメンバーは、"Yes/No" で答えられる質問をして、その職業が何かを当ててください。

Example:
A: OK. Do you work inside?
B: Sometimes.
C: Do you work 9 to 5?
B: No.
D: Do you work at night?
B: Sometimes.
E: Do you work at home?
B: No.
C: Do you sell* something?
B: No.
F: Do you drive a car?
B: Sometimes.
A: Do you wear a uniform?
B: Yes.
D: Are you a police officer?
B: Yes, that's right. Well done!

* sell 売る

Now it is your turn to play "What's My Job?" But first, you need to prepare some questions. Work in a group and add questions to the chart below.

以下の表にいくつか質問があります。グループ内で話し合いながら、新しい質問を作り、表に加えてください。

Do you …	Do you work …	Do you use …	Do you wear …	Is your job …
make a lot of money?	inside? in an office?	your hands? a computer?	a uniform?	dangerous?

Grammar 1

14

Time Expressions

時間を表す

I get up ***at*** 6:15 ***in*** the morning.

I eat lunch ***from*** 12:15 ***to*** 1:15 ***in*** the afternoon.

I arrive* home ***around*** 8:00 ***in*** the evening.

I work overtime ***until*** 9 p.m. ***on*** Fridays, so I get home ***late***.

I wake up ***early on*** weekdays, but I wake up ***late on*** weekends.

I check my smartphone ***before*** I go to bed ***at*** night.

I go to the gym ***after*** work ***on*** Mondays.

I go to bed ***late on*** Saturday night, so I sleep ***until*** noon* ***on*** Sunday.

* arrive 着く　noon 正午

▶Practice 7 Grammar Exercise: Time Expressions 文法問題：時間を表す

Complete the sentences using the time expressions in the box.

枠内から最も適切な単語を選んで空欄を埋めましょう。( ) 内の数字はその単語を何度使えるかを示しています。

on (3 times)	at (5 times)	in (4 times)	until (3 times)
after (2 times)	from	early	

1. I wake up ________ on weekdays* because I start work ________ 8 a.m., but I sleep ________ 10 or 11 a.m. ________ weekends.
2. I take a shower* ________ I wake up ________ the morning.
3. I work at the hospital ________ 11 p.m. to 7 a.m. four days a week. I get home* ________ 8 a.m. ________ the morning and go to bed ________ 10 a.m., ________ I eat breakfast. Then I sleep ________ 5:00 ________ the afternoon.
4. I usually go to bed ________ 11:00 ________ night ________ weekdays, but I stay up* ________ 2 a.m. ________ the morning ________ weekends.

* weekdays 平日　take a shower シャワーをあびる　get home 家に着く
stay up 夜遅くまで起きている　weekends 週末

▶Practice 8 Karen's Working Day カレンの一日

Karen is an office worker. She works in a company in Tokyo. Work in pairs. **Student A**: Look at Karen's schedule below. **Student B**: Look at her schedule in **Appendix 1**. Ask and answer questions to find the missing information in Karen's schedule.

カレンは企業に勤める会社員です。Student A は以下のカレンの予定を見て、Student B は Appendix 1 の予定を見てください。お互いに質問し合い，カレンの予定を埋めましょう。

Example:
Question: What does Karen do at 6 a.m.? Answer: She wakes up (at 6 a.m.).
Question: When does Karen wake up? Answer: (She wakes up) At 6 a.m.

Student A

Time	Activity
6 a.m.	Karen wakes up.
6:15 a.m.	Karen eats breakfast.
7 a.m.	
7:30 a.m. – 8:40 a.m.	Karen rides[*] the train.
	Karen arrives[*] at her office.
8:55 a.m.	Karen drinks a cup of tea.
9 a.m. – 9:30 a.m.	
9:30 a.m. – 9:45 a.m.	Karen calls the Osaka office.
	Karen works at her desk.
12 noon – 1 p.m.	Karen eats lunch.
1 p.m. – 2 p.m.	
2 p.m. – 5:30 p.m.	Karen works at her desk.
	Karen plans tomorrow's schedule.
6 p.m.	Karen leaves[*] the office.
6 p.m. – 6:10 p.m.	
6:10 p.m. – 7:20 p.m.	Karen goes home by train.
	Karen buys[*] food at the supermarket.
8 p.m.	Karen arrives home and cooks dinner.
9 p.m.	
10:30 p.m.	Karen takes a shower.
	Karen goes to bed.

[*] ride 乗る　arrive 着く　leave 出る、去る　buy 買う

Grammar 2

15

Present Continuous Tense (with "Wh" questions and answers)

現在進行形（"Wh" を使った質問と答え）

What **are** you **doing**?	I'**m writing** a report.
What'**s** he **doing**?	He'**s talking** to a customer*.
What'**s** she **doing**?	She'**s talking** on the phone.
Where **are** they **going**?	They'**re going** to a meeting.
Why'**s** she **leaving**?	She'**s going** home.

* customer（店などの）客

▶Practice 9 What Are They Doing? 彼らは何をしていますか？

Write answers to the questions, referring to the pictures. Use your imagination!

絵に関する質問に答えてください。想像力を使ってください！

1. What's he doing?

2. What's she doing?

3. What are they doing?

4. Why's he leaving?

5. Where's he going?

6. What's she carrying*?

7. What's she doing?

____

____

8. What's he doing?

____

____

9. Why's he smiling?

____

____

* carry 運ぶ

▶Practice 10 Find the Differences 違いを探そう

Student A: Look at the picture below. **Student B**: Look at the picture in **Appendix 2**. Tell your partner what is happening in your picture. Find nine differences between the two pictures.

Student A は以下の絵を、Student B は Appendix 2 の絵を見てください。パートナーにお互い自分の見ている絵を説明し、違いを 9 つ見つけましょう。

Example: Student A: In my picture, Mr. Kubo's reading a letter.
Student B: Oh, really? In my picture Mr. Kubo's reading a book.

* water a plant 植物に水をやる

▶Practice 11 Listening 16

Listen to a person talk about his dream job. He would like to be a travel writer. Write in the missing words.

旅行ライターになりたいと思っている人の話を聞いて、空欄を埋めましょう。

I'm a travel ______________. I work four days a week, ______________________________.
I usually write ______________________________ to about 1 p.m. Then I'm free to enjoy
the rest of* ____________________. I ______________________________ so I often go hiking.
I read after dinner and __________________________. I ______________________________.
I ________________ __________. It has ______________________________ a comfortable*
chair. I wear ______________________________. I ______________________________ and then
I write stories ______________________________. I ______________________________
it's exciting and I can ____. I also get to
____ the world.

* rest of ～ ～の残り comfortable 快適な

▶Practice 12 Presentation: Dream Job 理想の職業

Imagine you have the perfect job. Prepare a short presentation describing your daily life. Look at the description of the travel writer in **Practice 11** for ideas. You may include the following information:

今自分が理想の職業を持っていると仮定して、日々の仕事について説明してみましょう。Practice 11 の旅行ライターの話と、以下の情報を参考にして、プレゼンテーションを完成させましょう。

* What do you do? (Give details)
* What days and hours do you work?
* What is your day like?
* What do you like about your job?
* Do you wear special clothes*? Work outside? Drive or use special tools?
* How much money do you make?

Now share your dream job with your group. When you read, speak loudly and clearly and make eye contact with other group members.

それでは、グループのメンバーと理想の職業についてシェアしてみましょう。発表するときは、大きな声ではっきりと話し、アイコンタクトを忘れずに。

* clothes 服

Unit 3

What Does He Look Like?

見た目はどんな感じ？

Speaking

Practice the following dialogues with a partner. After you have practiced the model conversation a few times, substitute the underlined information with the words in the boxes.

以下の会話をパートナーと練習してください。数回練習したら，下線の部分を枠内の表現に言いかえて再度練習しましょう。

Dialogue 1 17

Yu: Tell me about your new boyfriend. What does he look like?

Ai: Well, he's medium* height*(1) and has short, brown(2) hair.

Yu: How old is he?

Ai: He's in his early 20's.*(3)

Yu: Is he good looking*?

Ai: I don't know about that. But he has big, brown eyes and freckles.*(4)

Yu: He sounds cute.

Ai: Yeah, I guess* he is.

1. short tall	2. blond black	3. mid 20's* late 20's*	4. sideburns* a mustache*

* medium 中くらいの　height 高さ　early 20's 20 代前半　good looking ルックスのよい
freckles そばかす　guess 〜だと思う　mid 20's 20 代半ば　late 20's 20 代後半
sideburns もみあげ　mustache 口ひげ

Dialogue 2 18

Rie: Tell me about your family, Doug.

Doug: I have a photo of them on my smart phone. Just a moment ... Ah, here it is.

Rie: Which one's your father?

Doug: He's the tall, slim*(1) man standing at the back. He has a mustache(2) and wears glasses.

Rie: And is that your sister?

Doug: No, that's my mom!

Rie: Your mom? Wow, she looks so young.

Doug: Yeah, she's ten years younger than my dad.

Rie: I love her long, black(3) hair.

1. thin*	2. beard*	3. curly, brown
muscular*	tattoo*	wavy*, blond

* slim 細い　thin 細い、薄い　muscular 筋肉たくましい　beard あごひげ
tattoo 入れ墨　wavy ウェーブのかかった、波状の

Grammar 1 19

Describing People

人について説明する

Subject + Verb (be) + Adjective	**Subject + Verb (have) + Noun**
He ***is*** good looking.	He ***has*** a mustache.
She ***is*** pretty.	She ***has*** a tattoo.
They ***are*** middle-aged*.	They ***have*** black hair.
Her hair ***is*** long.	She ***has*** long hair.

* middle-aged 中年の

Key Words: Describing People 人について説明する 20

1. Age: How old is she?

She's young.

They're middle-aged.

He's old/elderly.*

She's in her early teens*. / She's in her mid-thirties. / She's in her late*-fifties.

2. Height: How tall is he?

He's tall. He's short.

How tall are they?

She's short. They're medium (average*) height. She's tall.

* elderly 年配の teens (teenager) 10代の（ティーンエイジャー、10代の若者） late 後半の average 平均的な

3. Hair: What color is her hair?
Eyes: What color are her eyes?

She has black hair.
She has blue eyes.

She has red hair.
She has brown eyes.

She has brown hair.
She has green eyes.

She has blond hair.
She has blue eyes.

How long is her hair?

She has short hair.

She has medium-length hair.*

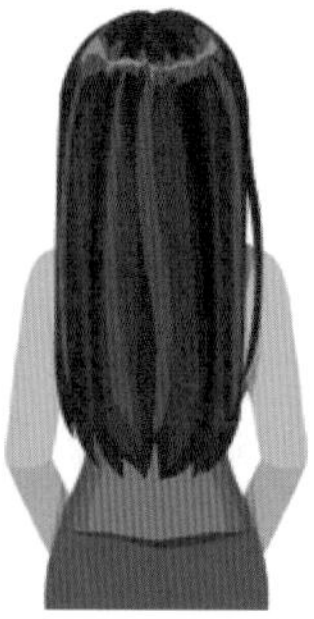

She has long hair.

She has straight hair.

She has wavy hair.

She has curly hair.

He's bald.*

* medium-length hair セミロング　bald 髪のない、禿げた

4. What do they look like?

They're handsome / good looking.

She's beautiful / good looking.

She's pretty / cute

He's thin / slim.

He's muscular.

They're large / overweight.*

He has a beard and a mustache.

5. Other

She wears glasses.

He has a tattoo.

He's in a wheelchair.*

* overweight 太った　　wheelchair 車いす

▶Practice 1 Verbs 動詞

Put the correct verb ("be" or "have") in the correct form in the sentences below.

空欄に be 動詞か have を適切な形にして入れましょう。

1. He ________________ medium height.
2. She ________________ curly, red hair.
3. They ________________ good looking.
4. My father ________________ bald and ________________ a beard.
5. My hair ________________ brown.
6. Those children ________________ cute.
7. I ________________ long, brown hair.
8. I ________________ big ears.

▶Practice 2 Matching 質問に合った答えをさがそう

Put the correct letters for the answers in the space.

1 ～ 10 までの質問に対する最も適切な答えを A から J の中から選びましょう。

_____ 1. Is he handsome?

_____ 2. How old is she?

_____ 3. What color is his hair?

_____ 4. Does he wear contact lenses*?

_____ 5. How tall is he?

_____ 6. What does she look like?

_____ 7. Is his hair brown?

_____ 8. How long is her hair?

_____ 9. Is he tall?

_____ 10. How old are they?

A. No, it's black.

B. They're both* elderly.

C. It's blond.

D. Yes, he is. He looks like a movie star.

E. She's medium height and thin and has short, brown hair.

F. No, he wears glasses.

G. No, he's short.

H. He's 168 centimeters* tall.

I. It's medium-length.

J. She's in her 20's.

* both 両方の contact lenses コンタクトレンズ centimeters センチメートル

▶Practice 3 Describing People 人について説明する

Describe the people in the pictures. Write whole sentences.

以下の絵について、主語、動詞を入れた説明文を作ってください。

1. How tall are they?

   Greg ______________________________.

   Sarah ______________________________.

   Cindy ______________________________.

Greg Sarah Cindy

A. B. C.

2. How old are they?

   A. ______________________________.

   B. ______________________________.

   C. ______________________________.

3. What color are her eyes?

   ______________________________.

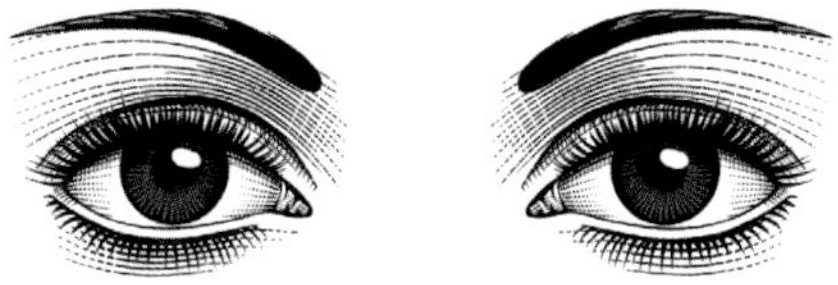

4. What does she look like?

   ____

   ______________________________.

5. What does he look like?

   ____

   ______________________________.

►Practice 4 Listening: Which One Is She? リスニング：その人は誰？ 21

Listen to the descriptions of nine people and write the number (from 1 to 9) in each box.

９人の人たちを説明する会話を聞いて、誰のことを説明しているのか１～９の番号を空欄に入れてください。

Christy   Nina   Allison   Layla   Mike   Nolan   Trevor   Roger   Tim

►Practice 5 Listening: Picture Drawing (1) リスニング：絵を描く（１） 22

Key Words

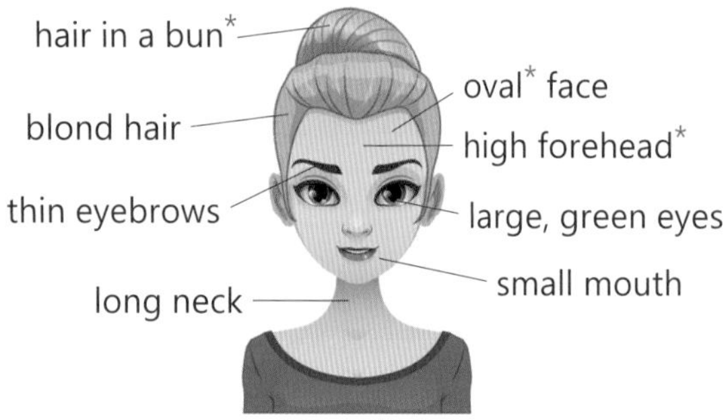

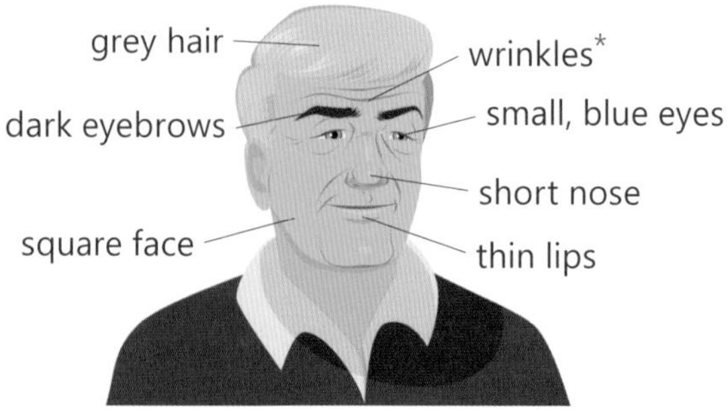

* round 丸い　thin 細い　eyebrows まゆげ　sideburns もみあげ　thick 太い
goatee ヤギひげ　in a bun 髪をお団子にした　oval 楕円形　forehead おでこ
wrinkles しわ　bangs 前髪　pigtails おさげ髪

Now, listen carefully and draw a picture of the person being described on a piece of paper. 23
人についての説明をよく聞いて、説明に合うよう絵を描いてみましょう。

dot 点　　stripe ストライプ

▶Practice 6 Pair Work: Picture Drawing (2) ペアワーク：絵を描く（2）

Draw a face in detail on a piece of paper. Don't show the picture to your partner. When finished, take turns describing your person's face. Your partner will draw the face you describe. The person drawing can ask questions. Use only English and have fun!
パートナーに見せないように、紙に顔を描いてください。描き終わったら絵を口頭でパートナーに説明し、パートナーはその情報をもとに顔を描きます。パートナーに色々質問しながら絵を描くことができます。ただし、日本語は使わないでくださいね！

Example: A: This person has a round face. He has a mustache. He has a big mouth.
B: Is his nose big, too?
A: No, it's normal size. But he has big ears. He has short blond hair.

Grammar

24

Comparatives and Superlatives
比較級と最上級

Comparatives	Superlatives
Bill's ***taller than*** Jane.	He's ***the tallest*** person I know.
Jane's ***shorter than*** Bill.	She's ***the shortest*** student in the class.
Mika's hair is ***curlier than*** mine.	Mika's hair is ***the curliest***.
Derek's ***more muscular*** than me.	Derek's ***the most muscular*** guy* in the class.
My hair is ***not as curly as*** Mika's.	

* guy 男の人

▶Practice 7 Comparatives and Superlatives 比較級と最上級

Complete the sentences below with the correct form of adjective.

適切な副詞（比較級か最上級）を使って以下の文章を完成させてください。

1. Tom is ______________________ (handsome) than Jack. He's probably* the ______________ ______________ (handsome) guy I've ever met!
2. This is a wonderful wedding ring. I think it's the __________________________ (beautiful) of all the rings in the store.
3. Yuichi is _______________ (fast) than me. In fact*, he's the ________________ (fast) runner in the school.
4. I'm ________________ (short) than my friend, Bob. I'm the ____________________ (short) person on my basketball team.
5. Ai is _______________ (smart*) than I am. Actually*, I think that she's the _______________ (smart) girl in our class.

* probably たぶん　In fact 実は、実際は　smart 賢い　actually 実は、実際は

▶Practice 8 Who Are You Talking About? 誰について話してるの？

Student A describes five people in **Picture A**. **Student B** should try to guess the person. **Student B** then looks at **Picture B** and describes five people with **Student A** guessing.

Student A は Picture A の絵から５人を選んでそれぞれを説明してください。Student B は誰のことを説明しているのかを当ててください。次に、Student B が Picture B の絵から５人を選んでそれぞれについて説明し、Student A は誰のことを説明しているのかを当てて下さい。

Picture A

Picture B

▶Practice 1 Writing: Describing People ライティング：人について説明する

Write some sentences describing each person below, talking about their work and their appearance.

以下の人たちについて、職業と見た目などを説明する文を書いてみましょう。

A. Blake B. Dana C. Yoji D. Gary E. Haru

A. ____.

____.

B. ____.

____.

C. ____.

____.

D. ____.

____.

E. ____.

____.

Review Units 1 - 3

▶Practice 2 Board Game ボードゲーム

To play the board game below, you will need to make groups. Follow the instructions.
以下のルールに従って、グループでボードゲームをしてみましょう。

1. Use small pieces of paper with your initials on them as markers.
   小さな紙に自分のイニシャルを書き，自分の駒にします。
2. Toss a coin or play 'rock, paper, scissors' to decide who goes first.
   コインを使って（またはジャンケンで）誰から始めるかを決めます。

START HERE

1. What's your first name? Do you like it? Why or why not?

2. What do you do?

3. Where do you live?

4. What do you do in your free time?

5. Do you have a part-time job? Tell us about it.

6. Do you have a pet? Tell us about him / her.

7. Do you like your classes? Why (not)?

8. How do you come to school?

9. What do you want to do in the future?

10. Do you want to work overseas in the future?

11. How many classes do you have every week?

12. How many people are there in your family?

13. What days do you come to school / university?

14. What does your father do?

15. What does your mother do?

• • •

3. Each player then takes turns by tossing a coin. If the coin lands face up, move two spaces. If the coin lands face down, move one space.
   順番にコインを投げ、表が出たら２マス、裏か出たら１マス進みます。
4. When you land on a space, answer the question. Answer any follow-up questions.
   出たマスの質問に答え，追加の質問にも答えます。

Useful expressions: 便利な表現：

I'll go first. 私から先にします。　Is it my turn? 私の番ですか？　It's your turn. あなたの番です。

22.
Imagine your dream partner (boyfriend / girlfriend). What does he / she look like?

23.
Introduce one of your friends (try to speak for 30 seconds without stopping*).

24.
Introduce yourself (try to speak for 30 seconds without stopping).

GOAL!

21.
What does your favorite actor look like?

20.
What does your mother look like?

19.
What does your father look like?

16.
What do your brothers and sisters do?

17.
Say the names of as many jobs as you can in 20 seconds*.

18.
Say as many adjectives* about appearance* as you can in 20 seconds.

* without stopping 止まらずに　second 秒　adjective 形容詞　appearance 見た目

Unit 4
Where Are You From?

どこから来たの？（出身地は？）

Speaking

Practice the following dialogues with a partner.

以下の会話をパートナーと練習しましょう。

Dialogue 1 25

Ms. Ota: Where are you from, Miguel?

Miguel: I'm from the Philippines.

Ms. Ota: Oh, really? I love the Philippines. What's your hometown*?

Miguel: Manila.

Ms. Ota: Oh, great! Do you like living in Japan?

Miguel: It's OK, but I miss* my family.

Dialogue 2 26

Misato: Where are you from, Pei?

Pei: I'm from Beijing*, China.

Misato: Oh, really? What's Beijing like?

Pei: It's a big city and it's very crowded*, like Tokyo. Do you live in Tokyo?

Misato: No, I don't. I live in Saitama.

Dialogue 3 27

Sharon: Where are you from, Awan?

Awan: My dad's from India, but my mom's Japanese. I was born in Japan.

Sharon: I want to go to India someday*. Do you speak Japanese?

Awan: Yes, I do.

Sharon: That's nice. I speak just a little.

*hometown 実家　miss さびしがる　Beijing 北京　crowded 混んでいる　someday いつか

Grammar

28

Questions and Answers in the Present Tense

現在形の質問と答え

Where **are** you from?	(I'**m** from) Canada.
What'**s** your hometown?	(It'**s**) Osaka.
What'**s** Tokyo like?	It'**s** exciting.
Do you **speak** English?	Yes, but just a little.
Are you Japanese?	No, I'**m** Korean.
What'**s** your future dream?	I **want** to speak English.
What do you **want** to do in the future?	I **hope** to go to Europe someday.
What do you **plan** to do tomorrow?	I **plan** to study.

▶Practice 1 Fill in the Blanks 穴埋め問題

Write in the correct form of the verbs in the conversation below.

カッコ内の動詞を最も適切な形に変えて空欄を埋めましょう。

Ms. Yokoyama: Hi, Carla. I ________________ (be) Mitsuko Yokoyama, Pedro's elementary school teacher.

Carla: It ________________ (be) nice ________________ ________________ (meet) you, Ms. Yokoyama.

Pedro: Nice ________________ ________________ (meet) you, too, Yokoyama Sensei.

Ms. Yokoyama: Please ________________ (call) me Mitsuko Sensei.

Pedro: OK, Mitsuko Sensei.

Ms. Yokoyama: And where ________________ (be) you from?

Carla: We ________________ (be) from Peru. We ________________ (speak) Spanish at home, but Pedro also ________________ (speak) English well. He ________________ (do) not speak Japanese, though.

►Practice 2 Nationality and Language 国籍と言語

Student A should look at the chart below. **Student B** should turn to **Appendix 3**. Take turns and ask questions. Write down the answers in the blanks below, as shown in the example.

Student A は下のチャートを見て、Student B は Appendix 3 を開いてください。交代で質問をし、空欄に正しい国名、言語を入れましょう。

Example: Student A: Where's Yelena from?
Student B: She's from Russia.
Student A: How do you spell "Russia"?
Student B: "R-U-S-S-I-A." What's her nationality*?
Student A: She's Russian. What language does she speak?
Student B: She speaks Russian.

* nationality 国籍

Student A

Name	Country	Nationality	Language
1. Yelena (she)	Russia	Russian	Russian
2. Charlotte (she)	United Kingdom		English
3. Min-jun (he)	Korea	Korean	
4. Mai (she)		Vietnamese	
5. Somchai (he)	Thailand		
6. Adam (he)		American	English
7. Yun (she)	China		Chinese
8. Miguel (he)		Brazilian	

▶Practice 3 Pair Work: The Story of Kim ペアワーク：Kim のストーリー

Work in pairs. **Student A** should stay on this page. **Student B** should turn to **Appendix 4**. Ask questions using the words in parentheses to get the information you need to fill in the spaces below.

Student A はこのページを見て、Student B は Appendix 4 を見てください。カッコ内の単語を使って質問しながら、空欄を埋めましょう。

Example: A: What does he like to do in his free time?
B: He likes to play ...

Student A

Kim is (1) ______________ (where / from). He's a student but he works part-time, too. He studies computer engineering at (2) ______________ (where / study). Kim is 20 years old and is a junior. His favorite class is called (3) ______________ (what / called). He wants to design new software programs in the future. Kim speaks (4) ______________ (what / Kim's main language), of course, but he also speaks a little English and a little Japanese. He plans to (5) ______________ (what / plan to do / next year) next year. He already has some Japanese friends that he met online. He's looking forward to* (6) ______________ (what / look forward to doing / next year) in Japan. He likes to play computer games and read comics in his free time.

*look forward to ～ ～を楽しみにする

▶Practice 4 Pair Work ペアワーク

Practice the following conversation using the substitute words below each picture.

それぞれの絵の情報を、以下の会話文にあてはめて練習してみましょう。

Somsak
Thailand
travel agent
play soccer

Example:

Somsak: Hi, I'm Somsak.
Reiko: Hi, Somsak. I'm Reiko. Where are you from?
Somsak: From Thailand.
Reiko: I see. And what do you do?
Somsak: I'm a travel agent*. How about you?
Reiko: I'm a graduate student*. So what do you like to do in your free time?
Somsak: I play soccer.

* travel agent 旅行会社　graduate student 大学院生

1. Liam
   Canada
   English teacher
   go hiking

2. Sophia
   Brazil
   fashion model
   go dancing

3. Yun
   China
   scientist*
   read

4. Ahmed
   Turkey
   reporter
   watch TV

5. Min-jun
   South Korea
   university student
   study Japanese

6. Sergei
   Russia
   businessman
   go out with* my wife

* scientist 科学者　go out with ～ ～と出かける

▶Practice 5 Reading リーディング

Culture is important to all of us. Each person is different, but the way we think, act*, and communicate also comes from our culture. We learn about our culture from our parents and other family members, from our friends, from school, from the media, and from many other places. When we travel overseas and meet people from other countries, we learn how different we are and how important culture is. When we hear the word "culture", we might* think about the cultures of different countries, for example, the culture of Japan or the culture of the U.S. But there are different cultures in each country, too. The people in Osaka are not the same as the people in Tokyo. Cultures also change: the culture of Japan today is different from the culture of Japan 50 or 100 years ago.

Some Japanese believe that Japanese culture is unique in the world, but every culture is different. We can learn a lot about people by studying their cultures and their way of thinking*.

* act ふるまう　might ～かもしれない　way of thinking 考え方

True or False 内容把握

Write "T" for true or "F" for false for each of the sentences below.

内容と一致している場合は "T"、一致していなければ "F" を入れましょう。

_____ 1. People in the same culture always have the same way of thinking and acting.

_____ 2. We learn about culture from parents, friends, TV, the internet, and many other places.

_____ 3. When we travel, we learn that people are the same.

_____ 4. One country can have different cultures.

_____ 5. Every culture is different.

►Practice 6 Pair Work: Global Village グローバルヴィレッジ

The world population is over 7.5 billion people (7,500,000,000!). If you think of the world as a global village with just 100 villagers, the variety of people is easier to imagine. Look at the information below. With a partner, put the correct numbers in the spaces.

世界には75億人が住んでいます。でも、もし地球上に人が100人しか住んでいなかったら、と仮定してみてください。世界の人々について色々なことが容易に想像できます。以下の情報を参考に、パートナーと、最も適切と思われる数字を空欄に入れましょう。

75　50　50　25

In the village, there are...

___ females*
___ males*
___ children
___ adults

* female 女性　male 男性

60　16　14　10

In the village, there are...

___ Africans
___ Asians
___ Europeans
___ people from the Americas*

* Americas 南北アメリカ大陸

31　23　16　~~15~~　8　7

In the village, there are...

___ Christians*
___ Muslims*
15 Hindus*
___ Buddhists*
___ people with no religion*
___ people who believe in other religions

* Christians キリスト教信者　Muslims イスラム教信者
Hindus ヒンズー教信者　Buddhists 仏教徒
religion 宗教

~~73~~　12　6　5　2　2

In the village, there are...

___ people who speak English
___ people who speak Chinese
___ people who speak Spanish
___ people who speak Russian
___ people who speak Japanese
73 people who speak other languages

Source: https://www.100people.org/statistics_100stats.php?section=statistics

▶Practice 7 Pair Work: Ideas About Japanese People ペアワーク：日本人について

Below are ideas some foreigners may have about Japanese people. In pairs, choose one idea below and share your own thoughts about what is true and not true. When you are done, present your ideas to the class. Imagine you are talking to foreigners who know little about Japan.

以下は外国人が持っているかもしれない日本人に対する印象です。パートナーといっしょに自分たちの考えをシェアし、それが本当かどうかを話し合ってみましょう。そのあとクラスでシェアし、外国人に話しているつもりで発表してみてください。

1. Japanese are workaholics*.

2. Japan is a man's country. Women follow* them.

3. Japanese are shy.

4. Japanese often wear kimono.

5. Japanese do not show their feelings.

6. Japanese are "nerdy*". They like animation and computer games.

* workaholic 働きすぎ　follow 後についていく　nerdy おたく

▶Practice 8 Listening リスニング 30

Listen to a person talk about Japanese houses. Fill in the missing words.

日本の家について話している人の話を聞いて、空欄を埋めましょう。

Let me tell you a little ____________________. Japanese homes ____________ ____________. People in cities often ____________________.
They are called *manshon*, but ____________________ Western mansions, which ____________________. Many families in suburbs* and towns live in houses, but ____________________. Most Japanese houses have a *genkan*, which is a ____________________ the front door. We ____________________ in this area and ____________________ slippers*. We never ____________________.

Traditional* ____________________ *tatami*, which are straw mats. They are comfortable ____________________. We take off* our slippers ____________________ *tatami*. Japanese ____________________ *futons* that are put on* *tatami*. Today, Japanese homes have fewer* *tatami* rooms, and ____________________ Western-style* beds. In fact, ____________________ are Western-style homes.

* suburb 郊外　slippers スリッパ　traditional 伝統的な　take off 脱ぐ
put on 履く、身に着ける　fewer より少ない　western-style 西洋風の

▶Practice 9 Presentation: Life in Japan プレゼンテーション：日本での生活

Imagine you will give a talk to foreigners who know little about Japan. Prepare a short presentation describing some part of Japanese life. Look at **Practice 8** as an example. You may choose one of the following topics, but anything about Japanese life is fine!

日本のことをあまり知らない外国人に、日本についてのプレゼンテーションを行います。日本での生活について短いプレゼンテーションを作りましょう。Practice 8 と以下のトピックを参考にしてください。自分でトピックを考えても構いません。

Possible topics:

- A Japanese holiday
- A type of Japanese food
- Traditional Japanese clothes
- A popular sport in Japan (baseball, soccer, *sumo*, etc.)
- Japanese education (university, entrance examinations*, English study, *juku*, etc.)
- A famous place in Japan (Kyoto, Kamakura, etc.)

* entrance examination 入学試験

Unit 5

Likes and Dislikes

好き嫌い

Speaking

Practice the following dialogues with a partner. After you have practiced the model conversation a few times, substitute the underlined information with the words in the boxes.

以下の会話をパートナーと練習してください。数回練習したら，下線の部分を枠内の表現に言いかえて再度練習しましょう。

Dialogue 1 31

Kishika: I have two tickets for the Giants game this evening. Do you want to come?

Paolo: Oh, yes. I love(1) baseball.

Kishika: I do, too.(2) Let's go together, then.

Paolo: And before the game starts, let's get something to eat.

Kishika: That's a good idea.

Paolo: How about Indian food?

Kishika: Sorry, but I don't really like(3) spicy food.

Paolo: Really? I do.(4) OK, then, let's go to the new Italian restaurant near the station.

1. I really like I'm crazy about*	2. So do I. So am I.	3. I'm not crazy about I can't stand*	4. I like it. I love it.

*crazy about～ ～に夢中　　stand 我慢する

Dialogue 2 32

Alex: Do you want to watch a movie on TV tonight?

Sandra: That's a good idea. What's on*?

Alex: Well, we could watch "The Living Dead."

Sandra: Oh, no! I hate* horror movies.

Alex: Oh, really? I like them. Well then*, how about "Tokyo Love Story"?

Sandra: That sounds* better. I like romantic comedies*.

Alex: So do I.*

*what's on 何を (TV で) やってる?　　hate ひどく嫌う　　well then じゃあ　　sound ～だと思う、～そう
romantic comedy (rom-com) ロマンチックコメディ　　so do I 私も

Grammar 1

33

Expressing Likes and Dislikes* (1) 好き嫌いを表現する

Strongly* like

I'm crazy about computer games.
I love dogs.
I really like tennis. / I like tennis a lot.
I like Korean pop music.
I'm not crazy about computer games.
I don't like volleyball very much.
I dislike Korean dramas.
I hate *natto*.
I can't stand that actor.

Strongly dislike

* dislike 嫌いなこと　　strongly 非常に

▶Practice 1 Writing: Questions and Answers ライティング：自分のことについて答えよう

Write short answers that are true for you, like the example below.

自分のことについて以下の例を参考にして答えましょう。

Example: Do you like dogs? Yes, I do. I love them.

1. Do you like sports? ______________________
2. Do you like *natto*? ______________________
3. Do you like cats? ______________________
4. Do you like tests? ______________________
5. Do you like video games? ______________________

Grammar 2

34

Expressing Likes and Dislikes (2) 好き嫌いを表現する

What kind of* music do you like?	I'm really into* rock music.
What's your favorite kind of music?	I like J-pop best.
Who's your favorite singer?	I don't have a favorite singer.
What kind of movies do you dislike?	(I dislike) Horror movies.
What do you think of K-pop?	It's OK*.
How do you like jazz?	I don't really like it.

* what kind of ～ どんな種類の　　be + into ～ ～にはまっている　　OK まあまあ

▶Practice 2 Entertainment Survey アンケート

First, write answers to the questions under "**You**". When you are done, ask the questions to a partner and write his or her answers under "**Your Partner**." Write two of your own questions.

"You" の下に左側の質問に対する答えを書き、そのあとパートナーに質問し、"Your Partner" の下にその答えを書きましょう。

	You	Your Partner
1. What kind of music do you like?		
2. What kind of music do you dislike?		
3. Who's your favorite singer?		
4. What's your favorite band?		
5. What kind of movies do you like?		
6. What kind of movies do you dislike?		
7.		
8.		

Grammar 3

35

Agreeing and Disagreeing 同意する、同意しない

Agreeing 同意する

A: I'm crazy about romance movies.
B: So am I.

A: I love hip hop.
B: So do I.

A: I like pancakes.
B: So do I.

A: I don't like blue cheese.
B: Neither do I*.

A: I hate horror movies.
B: So do I.

A: I can't stand rap music.
B: Neither can I.

Disagreeing 同意しない

A: I'm crazy about romance movies.
B: Oh, really? I'm not. I don't like them.

A: I love hip hop.
B: Oh, I don't.

A: I like pancakes.
B: I don't.

A: I don't like blue cheese.
B: Oh, I do. I love it.

A: I hate horror movies.
B: Oh really? I love them.

A: I can't stand rap music.
B: Really? I love it.

* neither do I 私も〜ない

▶Practice 3 Pair Work: Likes and Dislikes ペアワーク：好き嫌い

Write the name of different things in the spaces below. When done, share your sentences with your partner, who will respond, as below:

以下の空欄に名詞（もの、人、場所など）を入れましょう。書き終わったら、パートナーはそれについてどう思うか、意見を述べましょう。以下の例を参考にしてください。

Example: Student A: I don't like horror movies.
Student B: Neither do I.

1. I'm crazy about ______________________.
2. I love ______________________.
3. I like ______________________.
4. I don't like ______________________.
5. I hate ______________________.
6. I can't stand ______________________.

▶Practice 4 Pair Work: Food Likes and Dislikes ペアワーク：食べ物の好き嫌い

Look at the different kinds of food below. Write the name of the food and which country it comes from, as in the example.

絵を見て、食べ物の名前とその食べ物の国を書きましょう。以下の例を参考にしてください。

Example:

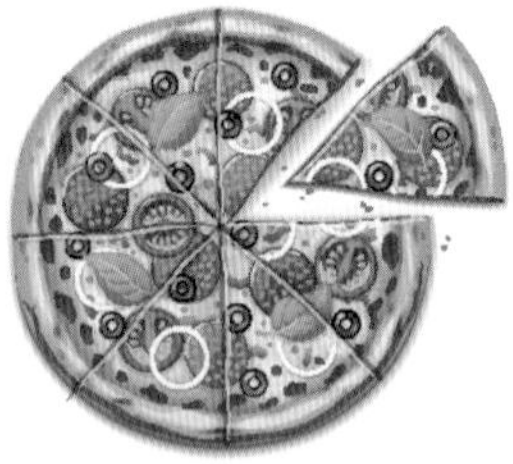

Food: This is a pizza.
Kind of food: It's Italian. / It comes from Italy.

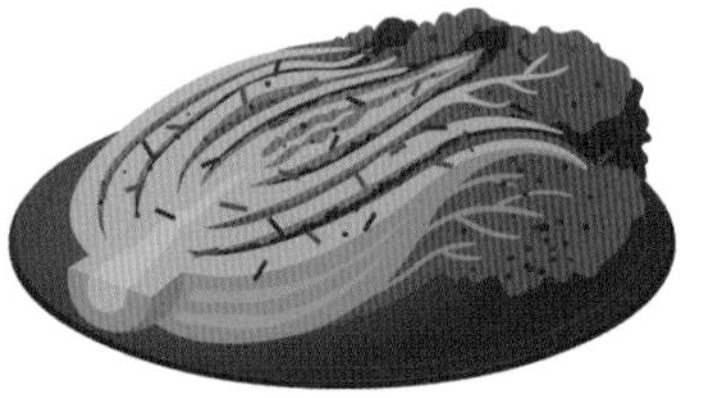

1. ______________________
____

2. ______________________
____

3. ______________________
____

4. ______________________
____

5. ______________________
____

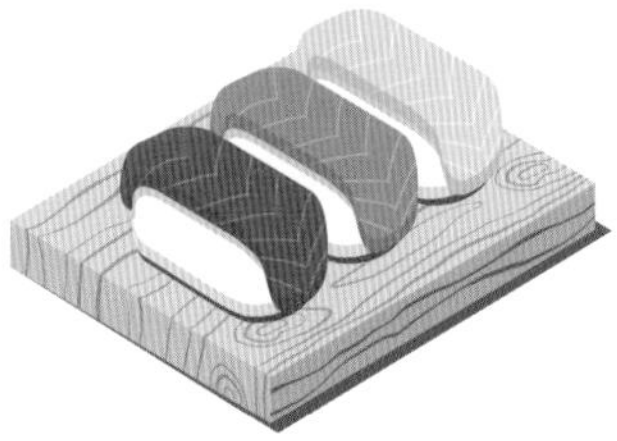

6. ______________________
____

Now take turns talking about each food on page 48 and the other student gives a response, as in the example below:

48ページにあるそれぞれの食べ物に関してコメントし、それについてパートナーと順番に意見を述べましょう。以下の例を参考にしてください。

Example: Student A: I like pizza.
Student B: Oh, I don't.

Grammar 4

36

Gerunds and Infinitives

動名詞と不定詞

So far, we learned to talk about likes and dislikes using nouns as objects (O).
名詞を目的語として、物、人、場所などの好き嫌いを表す練習をしてきました。

I like tennis. (S + V + O)

We can also talk about likes and dislikes for different kinds of activities.
動詞を目的語にして、行動や活動などの好き嫌いを表すこともできます。

I like **to play** tennis.	(infinitive)
I like **playing** tennis.	(gerund)
I don't like **to do** chores[*].	(infinitive)
I hate **taking** tests.	(gerund)
Do you like **studying** / **to study**?	(gerund / infinitive)

* chores 雑用、家事

▶Practice 5 Writing: Questions and Answers ライティング：自分のことについて答えよう

Write short answers that are true for you.

自分のことについて答えましょう。

Example: Do you like cooking? Yes, I do. I love it.

1. Do you like going to the dentist[*]? ________________
2. Do you like playing computer games? ________________
3. Do you like reading novels[*]? ________________
4. Do you like doing chores? ________________

* dentist 歯医者　novels 小説

▶Practice 6 Listening リスニング 37

Listen to the following conversation and write in the missing words.

会話文を聞いて空欄を埋めましょう。

Dana: What kind of things do you ____________________ free time?

Haru: Well, let me see. I ____________________ a lot, especially* action movies.

Dana: ______________. I ____________________ movies in theaters*.

Haru: ______________. I prefer* watching them on TV. I ____________________ sports on TV.

Dana: I don't. To be honest*, that's boring* for me. I ____________________, though*.

Haru: I ______________. Can you teach me ______________?

Dana: Sure*, but I ____________________ this month.

Haru: ______________. I have to study for tests.

*especially 特に　theater 映画館、劇場　prefer 好き　to be honest 正直なところ　boring つまらない　though（文末に使われた場合）～だけどね　sure もちろん

▶Practice 7 Writing ライティング

First, write down your feelings about the things or activities below. Use as many different phrases as you can (I like, I really like, I don't like, I hate, etc.). Also, use the verbs in some sentences to make gerunds or infinitives.

以下の活動やもの、生きものに対して自分がどう思うかを話してみましょう。できるだけ多くの異なるフレーズ (I like, I really like, I don't like, I hate, etc.) を使ってください。また、不定詞や動名詞などの動詞も使ってみてください。

Example: I don't like listening to classical music. (listen)

1. ______________________________ (bugs)　2. ______________________________ (puppies)

3. ______________________________ (study)

4. ______________________________ (exercise)

5. ______________________________ (shop)

6. ______________________________ (fly)

7. ______________________________ (do chores)

8. ______________________________ (broccoli)

Pair Work ペアワーク

Now, read your sentences and see if your partner agrees or disagrees with you.

自分とパートナーの意見が同じかどうか聞いてみましょう。

▶Practice 8　Survey: Entertainment　アンケート：娯楽芸能

Choose one type of entertainment to write a survey about (sports, music, TV, video games, etc.). Write five questions. Then ask your questions to at least five students in the class. Finally, prepare to share what you learned in your survey.

娯楽芸能のうち一つ選んで（スポーツ、音楽、テレビ、ビデオゲームなど）それに関してアンケートを作ってみましょう。例を参考にして質問を５問作り、最低５人のクラスメイトに聞いてみましょう。最後にそのアンケートからわかったことをシェアしてください。

Example:　**About Music**
What kind of music do you like?
Who's your favorite musician? / What's your favorite band?
Do you go to concerts?
When do you listen to music?
How often* do you listen to music?

*often　頻繁に

▶Practice 9　Group Work: Guessing Game　グループワーク：誰のことかな？

Write down your answers to the following questions on a piece of paper. Do not write your name on the paper. The teacher will collect your answers so the class can play a guessing game.

以下の質問の答えを紙に書いてください。先生が集めますが自分の名前は書かないでください。質問の答えから誰が書いたのか当てましょう。

1. What's your favorite character (animation, prefecture character*, etc.)?
2. What food do you like the best (main dish*, snack, dessert)?
3. What food do you dislike or hate?
4. What's your favorite free-time activity?
5. What kind of music do you like?
6. Who's your favorite famous* person (actor, singer, writer, etc.)?

*prefecture character　県のマスコットキャラクター　　main dish　主菜　　famous　有名な

Unit 6

What's She Like?

彼女ってどんな人？

Speaking

Practice the following dialogues with a partner. After you have practiced the model conversation a few times, substitute the underlined information with the words in the boxes.

以下の会話をパートナーと練習してください。数回練習したら，下線の部分を枠内の表現に言いかえて再度練習しましょう。

Dialogue 1 38

Hua: Did you meet the new English teacher yet?

Shun: No. What's she like?

Hua: Well, I hear* that she's friendly(1) but a little stubborn*(2).

Shun: Oh, really? I hope I like her class.

Hua: Yeah, me too.

1. intelligent* energetic* a good listener*	2. nervous* forgetful* strict*

*I hear that ～ ～らしい　stubborn 頑固な　intelligent 知的な　energetic エネルギッシュな、元気な　good listener 聞き上手　nervous 緊張した、神経質な　forgetful 忘れっぽい　strict 厳しい

Dialogue 2 39

Akane: What do you think of* Megan, the new student?

Li: She seems* friendly, but she talks too much and doesn't listen.

Akane: Yes, that's my experience*, too. I think she's a little selfish*.

Li: She hangs out* a lot with Mari. Mari is very patient* with her.

Akane: I know. Mari's kind to everybody.

*think of ～ ～と思う　seem ～に見える　experience 経験　selfish 自分勝手な　hang out 出かける　patient 我慢強い

Dialogue 3 40

Min: What's your personality* like, Gen?

Gen: Well, I think I'm energetic and positive*, but I'm forgetful. And I sometimes get emotional*.

Min: You're also very intelligent and well-organized*.

Gen: Do you think so*? Thank you.

Min: I'm more negative* than you. And I'm too nervous*.

Gen: But you're sensitive* and you're also a good listener.

*personality 性格　positive 前向きな　emotional 感情的な　well-organized きちんとした、几帳面な
do you think so? そう思う?　negative 否定的な、ネガティブな　nervous 神経質な　sensitive 繊細な

▶Practice 1 Words to Talk about Personality 性格を表す表現

Put the words in the box under the correct picture.

次の絵を最もよく表す表現を枠内から選びましょう。

positive　stubborn　negative　friendly　energetic
forgetful　honest　emotional / sensitive　nervous
intelligent　organized　a good listener

1. ________　2. ________　3. ________　4. ________

5. ________　6. ________　7. ________　8. ________

9. ________________ 10. ________________ 11. ________________ 12. ________________

▶Practice 2 Good Points and Bad Points 長所と短所

Look at the list of personality traits below. Put the opposite meanings for the traits listed in the chart.

表に書き込まれた単語と反対の意味を表す単語を、枠内から選んで書き入れましょう。

extroverted 外向的な careless 不注意な stingy けちな
emotional 感情的な negative 否定的な active 活動的な
practical 合理的 independent 独立心のある、自立した
illogical 非論理的な flexible 柔軟性のある honest 正直な
interesting おもしろい friendly 親しみやすい humble 謙虚な

1.		dishonest
2.	careful	
3.		boring
4.		passive
5.	arrogant	
6.	logical	
7.		unfriendly
8.	introverted	
9.		unrealistic
10.		calm
11.	positive	
12.		dependent
13.	generous	
14.		stubborn

▶Practice 3 Comparatives and Superlatives (1) 比較級と最上級（1）

Write three sentences, the first with an appropriate adjective, then the second sentence with the comparative and the third with the superlative form. You may want to look back at page 31.

まず、形容詞の原級を使った文を作り、そのあと比較級、最上級を使った文を作りましょう。31 ページを参考にしてください。

Example:

Mt. Fuji (3,776 m)

Mt. McKinley (6,190 m)

Mt. Everest (8,848 m)

(high) Mt. Fuji is *high*. Mt. McKinley is *higher*. Mt. Everest is the *highest*.

Abdul (183 cm)

Koji (187 cm)

Lan (194 cm)

1. (tall) ____________________

____

Stephen Hawkins (IQ 160)

Albert Einstein (IQ 175)

Gary Kasparov (IQ 190)

2. (intelligent) ____________________

____

Godzilla

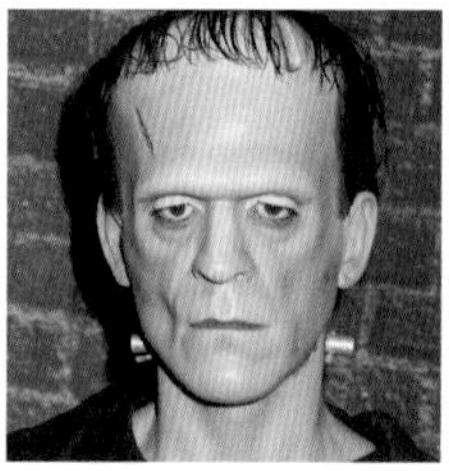
Frankenstein

Dracula

3. (scary*) ____________________

____

* scary 怖い

Grammar

41

More on Comparatives

～よりずっと、～と同じくらい

① You can use "much" to add emphasis.
比較級を使った文の意味をより強調したいときは、"much" を使います。

Mel is ***much*** taller than Cheri. Mel は Cheri より**ずっと**背が高い。

The movie is ***much*** more exciting than the novel. その映画は小説より**ずっと**おもしろい。

② When you compare two things that are equal in some way, you can use "as ～ as."
as + adjective + as ～と同じくらい / not as + adjective + as ～ほど～ではない

Tom is ***as tall as*** his father. トムは彼の父親と**同じくらい**の背の高さだ。

Tom is ***not as tall as*** his brother. トムは彼の兄**ほど**背が高く**ない**。

▶Practice 4 Comparatives and Superlatives (2) 比較級と最上級 (2)

Complete the sentences below with the correct form comparative or superlative of the adjective. Try to make the sentence by using "much ～ than," "the + superlative," "as ～ as."

"much ～ than"、"the+ 最上級 "、"as ～ as" を使い、カッコ内の形容詞を最も適切な形にして空欄に入れましょう。

1. Patrick is ________________ (intelligent) than me. In fact*, he's ________________ ________________ (intelligent) person in our class.
2. Ms. Peterson is ________________ (interesting) than Mr. Cook. Actually*, I think that she's ________________ (interesting) teacher I know.
3. My new boyfriend is ________________ (kind) than Naoki. He's ________________ ________________ (kind) guy I've ever dated*!
4. Kei is so forgetful. I can't rely on* her to do anything. You're ________________ (reliable*) than her. In fact, you're ________________ (reliable) person I know.
5. Richard always tells the truth*. He's ________________ (honest) than me. I think he's ________________ (honest) person I've ever met.
6. My sister Maya is ________________ (stubborn) than Yasuko. She's ________________ ________________ (stubborn) as I am, and I'm really stubborn.
7. My brother is ________________ (smart) than me, but he's not ________________ ________________ (smart) as my sister.
8. Max is ________________ (careful*) than Richard.

*in fact /actually 実は　date 付き合う　rely on ～ ～に頼る　reliable 信頼できる
tell the truth 本当のことを言う　careful 用心深い

▶Practice 5 Which is the Best? 一番いいのはどれ？

Read the following questions and then fill in the blanks with the correct superlative form of the adjectives given.

カッコ内の形容詞の原級を参考に、最上級を使った文に書き変えましょう。

Example: Where's <u>the best</u> (good) place to buy clothes?

1. Who's ______________________ (good) athlete* in Japan?
2. Who's ______________________ (handsome) actor?
3. Who's ______________________ (beautiful) actress?
4. Who's ______________________ (funny*) person in this class?
5. Which computer game is ______________________ (interesting)?
6. Who's ______________________ (talented*) singer in Japan?
7. What's ______________________ (delicious) food for you?
8. Which of your classes is ______________________ (difficult)?
9. What's ______________________ (exciting*) movie you've ever seen?
10. Who's ______________________ (important*) person in your life?

Now ask and answer the questions with a partner.

それでは、パートナーと質問しあいましょう。

* athlete スポーツ選手　funny おかしな　talented 才能のある　exciting わくわくする　important 大事な

▶Practice 6 Picture Drawing 絵を描こう

Listen to your teacher's instructions and draw a picture on a piece of paper.

先生の説明に沿って、別の紙に絵を描きましょう。

▶Practice 7 Reading: Personality リーディング：性格

Read the passage below and fill in the missing words from the choices given in the box.

次の文の空欄に入る最も適切な単語を、枠内から選びましょう。

people　friends　important　media　debate 議論
psychologists 心理学者　characteristics 特質

People have different personalities and ____________________. Where does our personality come from? Some ____________________ who do research* say that the environment* is the main source* of our personality. The environment includes* all the ____________________ in our lives*, such as* our family, our ____________________, and our teachers. It also includes our culture and the ____________________, such as the internet and TV. Other psychologists believe that our DNA has the biggest effect* on our personality. This ____________________ is often* called the "nature (genetics*) or nurture* (environment)"* argument*. Most psychologists today believe that both genetics and life experience* are ____________________ in making people's personality.

* research 研究　environment 環境　main source 主な要因　include 含む　lives 生活
such as ～ ～のような　effect 影響　often 頻繁に　genetics 遺伝的特徴
nurture 育ち　"nature or nurture"「人は遺伝子によって決まるのか、環境によって決まるのか」
argument 議論　life experience 人生経験

True or False 内容把握

Write "T" for true or "F" for false for each of the sentences below.

次の文が内容と一致している場合は "T"、一致していなければ "F" を入れましょう。

_____ 1. Most people have similar* personalities.

_____ 2. The environment has no effect on our personality.

_____ 3. Our family and friends help make our personality.

_____ 4. The "nature or nurture" argument is about what things effect our personality most.

_____ 5. Most psychologists believe that our personality is made by both our DNA and our environment.

* similar 似た

▶Practice 8 What Kind Of Person Are You? あなたはどんな人？

Use the survey below to find someone who answers "yes" to your questions. Write your own questions for numbers nine and ten. Talk to as many people as you can. If possible, ask follow-up questions.

表の質問に "Yes" と答えられる人を見つけたら、その人の名前を右側の欄に記入してください。空欄にはすべて異なる人の名前を記入してください。9 と 10 は、自分で質問を作って聞いてみましょう。できるだけ多くの人に聞いて、できれば追加の質問もしてみましょう。

Question	Name
1. Are you calm* most of the time?	
2. Do you like to play sports?	
3. Do you like meeting new people?	
4. Are you sometimes stubborn?	
5. Do you sometimes cry when you watch a sad movie?	
6. Do you want an easy job with a low salary*?	
7. Do you want a difficult job with high salary?	
8. Do you want to live in a foreign country*?	
9.	
10.	

* calm 落ち着いた　salary 給料　foreign country 外国

▶Practice 9 Imagine 想像してみよう

Complete the sentences below. Any answer is OK, so feel free to use your imagination. After you have finished, share your answers in a group.

「もし自分が～だったら」という文を完成させ、グループ内でシェアしましょう。

1. If I were a color, I would be ______________________________.
2. If I were an animal, I would be ______________________________.
3. If I were an object*, I would be ______________________________.
4. If I were a kind of food or drink, I would be ______________________________.
5. If I could choose* any job, I would be ______________________________.

* object もの　　choose 選ぶ

▶Practice 10 Listening: What Do You Know? リスニング：知ってますか？ 42

Listen to some questions. Then write down the answers in complete sentences. Use the words in the box.

質問を聞いて、文章で答えてください。枠内の単語を使いましょう。

Nouns:	lake	tower	ocean*	country	runner
	mountain	rock	river	wooden building*	
Adjectives:	deep*	hard			

* ocean 海　　wooden building 木造のビル　　deep 深い

Example: Question: What is the biggest city in the US?
Answer: New York is the biggest city.

* population 人口

1. ______________________________.
2. ______________________________.
3. ______________________________.
4. ______________________________.
5. ______________________________.
6. ______________________________.
7. ______________________________.
8. ______________________________.
9. ______________________________.
10. ______________________________.

▶Practice 11 Group Work: Who Am I? 私は誰？

You will have the name of a famous person put on your back. Ask "yes/no" questions to get information to find out who you are. Ask one question to one person and then move to another person. When you find out who you are, tell the teacher.

グループ内の一人が、自分の背中に有名人の名前を書いた紙を貼られます。紙を貼られた人は、グループ内の他のメンバーが、"Yes/No" で答えられる質問をするので、自分が誰かを当ててください。

Example:
A: Am I a famous singer?
B: No, you're not.
A: Am I an actor?
C: Yes, you are.
A: Am I a man?
D: No, you're not.
A: Am I Japanese?
E: No, you're not.

Before you begin, prepare some questions to ask. Work with a group to make good questions in the chart below.

以下の表にいくつか質問があります。グループ内で話し合いながら、新しい質問を作り、表に加えてください。

Am I ...	Do I ...
still alive? / dead?	belong to a band? act in a TV drama?

Review Units 4 - 6

▶Practice 1 Crossword クロスワード

Work in pairs.. **Student A**: Look at this page. **Student B**: Turn to **Appendix 5**. Give hints to help your partner guess the words that you can see in your half of the crossword. But do not say the actual words in your hints. Then listen to your partner and write in the words that he / she is describing.

ペアになって，Student A はこのページを，Student B は Appendix 5 を見てください。それぞれのクロスワードですでに埋まっている単語をパートナーにあててもらいます。ヒントを出し合い，お互いのクロスワードの空欄を埋めましょう。 答えを言ってしまわないように気を付けて。

Example: A: What's 9 down?
B: It's a house, a place that people live in with their families.
A: A home?
B: That's right! Now, what's 2 across?
B: It's the same as "personality".

Student A

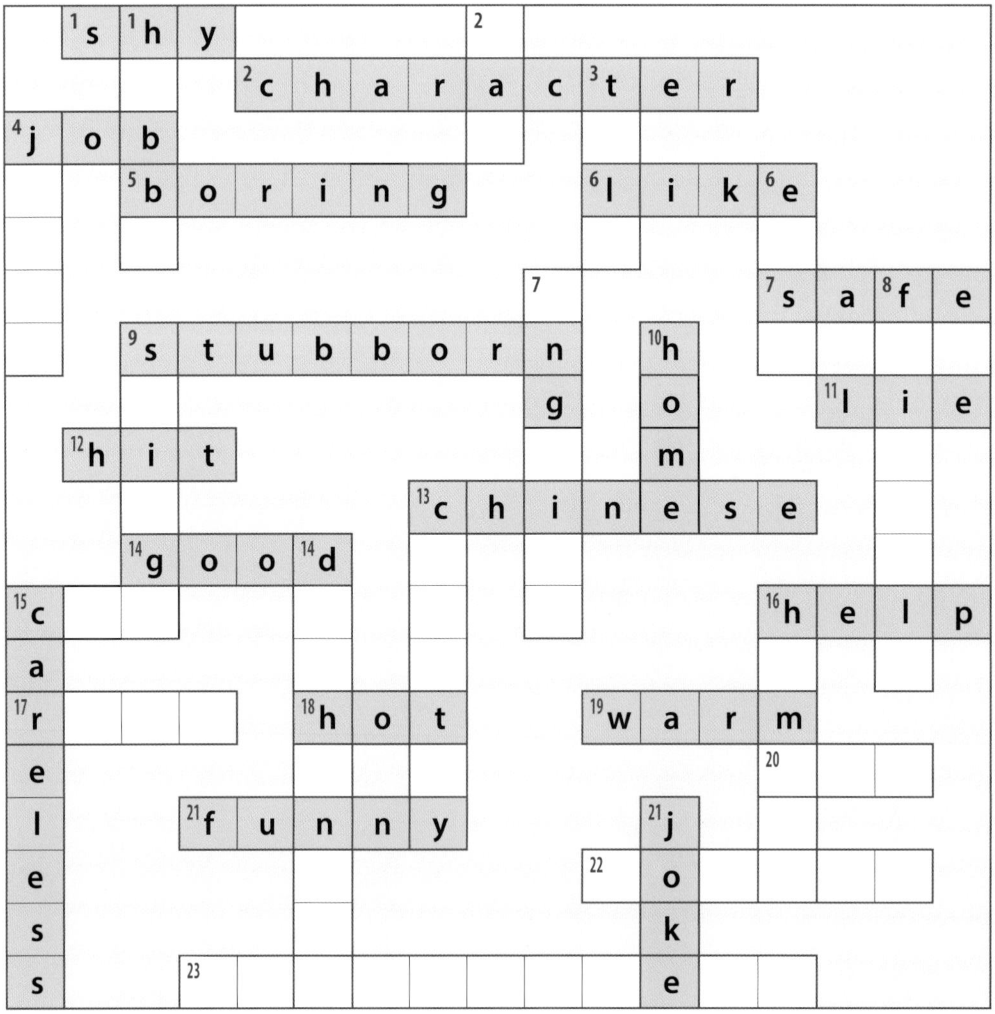

▶Practice 2 Listening: Date Your Dream リスニング：理想のデートの相手

Key Words 🎧43

active 活動的な　beach　look forward to ～ ～を楽しみにする　relaxed
easy going 気楽な、のんきな　guy 男の人　calm 落ち着いた　gardening
spend (time)（時間を）使う　go out (to eat)（食べに）出かける　noisy（音が）うるさい
salesman　pretty かなり　shy　actually 実際　animation
nerd オタク　I don't mind　nurse　elementary school　divorced 離婚した
nervous　emotional　excited　confident 自信のある　boastful いばった

Tina is on a show called "Date Your Dream." Listen to three men and Tina talk about themselves. Takes notes in the chart below. Which man is the best date for Tina? 🎧44

Tina は "Date Your Dream" というテレビ番組に出演しています。3 人の男性と Tina との会話を聞いて下の表にメモを取りましょう。Tina に一番合う相手は誰でしょう？

	Naoki	Sid	Ernie	Tina
Job				
Age				
Personality				
Hobbies and interests				
Likes				
Dislikes				

Unit 7

Tell Me About Your Family

家族について教えて

Speaking

Practice the following dialogues with a partner.

以下の会話をパートナーと練習しましょう。

Dialogue 1 45

Derick: Can you tell me about your family, Kaho?

Kaho: Sure. There are four of us, my father, my mother, my brother, and me.

Derick: How old is your brother?

Kaho: He's in the first year of high school, so he's 16 now. He's four years younger than me.

Derick: Do you get along with* him?

Kaho: Yeah, most of the time*. He's very responsible*, unlike* me.

Derick: That's not true*, Kaho! You're a very good person.

*get along with ～ ～と気が合う　most of the time たいてい　responsible 責任感のある
unlike ～ ～と違って　That's not true. そんなことはない

Dialogue 2 46

Kaho: What does your father do, Derick?

Derick: He's a businessman. He works for a company* in Tokyo.

Kaho: And your mother?

Derick: She's a doctor. She works in a hospital. My parents have to work until* late, so I'm often home alone*. What about your parents, Kaho?

Kaho: They're both counselors. My mother's a university counselor and my father works in a mental hospital*.

*company 会社　until ～ ～まで　alone 一人　mental hospital 精神科病院

Dialogue 3 47

Kaho: Is your father strict*?

Derick: Yes, but he's fair*. I respect* him.

Kaho: How about your mother?

Derick: She's very funny. She has a great sense of humor*.

Kaho: Your family sounds wonderful. My parents are too strict and often get angry* at me.

Derick: Do you have a curfew*?

Kaho: Yes, I must be home by* 10 p.m., even* on weekends. It drives me crazy*!

*strict 厳しい　fair 公平な　respect 尊敬する　sense of humor ユーモアのセンス
get angry 怒る　curfew 門限　by (time) （時間）までに　even ～でさえ
drive (someone) crazy （誰かを）怒らせる、イライラさせる

Grammar 1 48

There is…There are…

～がある / ～がいる（単数・複数）

How many people are there in your family?	(There are) Five.
How many students are there in your class?	(There are) 26.
Are there any questions?	No, there aren't.
Is there any homework?	Yes, there is.
Is there an English test next week?	Yes, there is. There's one on Friday.

▶Practice 1 Matching 質問に合った答えをさがそう

Put the letter for the correct answer next to each question.

1～6までの質問の答えとして、最も適切なものをA～Fから選びましょう。

____ 1. How many people are there in your family?
____ 2. How many units does this book have?
____ 3. Is there any homework?
____ 4. Is there a test on Monday?
____ 5. Is there a bank near here?
____ 6. Are there any more questions?

A. Yes, we have to write a report.
B. Yes, I'd like to ask one.
C. There are just three. I'm an only child*.
D. Yes, there's one on Main Street.
E. Yes, but I haven't studied for it yet.
F. It has 12.

*only child ひとりっ子

Key Words

Family Members 家族、親戚

49

mother　father　aunt 叔母　uncle 伯父　grandfather　grandmother
grandson 孫息子　granddaughter 孫娘　son 息子　daughter 娘　brother
sister　cousin いとこ　niece 姪　nephew 甥　husband 夫　wife 妻
stepfather 継父　stepmother 継母　parent 親　mother-in-law 義理の母親
father-in-law 義理の父親　brother-in-law 義理の兄弟　sister-in-law 義理の姉妹

▶Practice 2 Family Tree (Part 1) 家系図 パート1

Look at Kevin's family tree. Write the correct Key Words in the spaces below.

空欄を埋めて、ケヴィンの家の家系図を完成させましょう。ケヴィンから見た家族関係を書いて下さい。

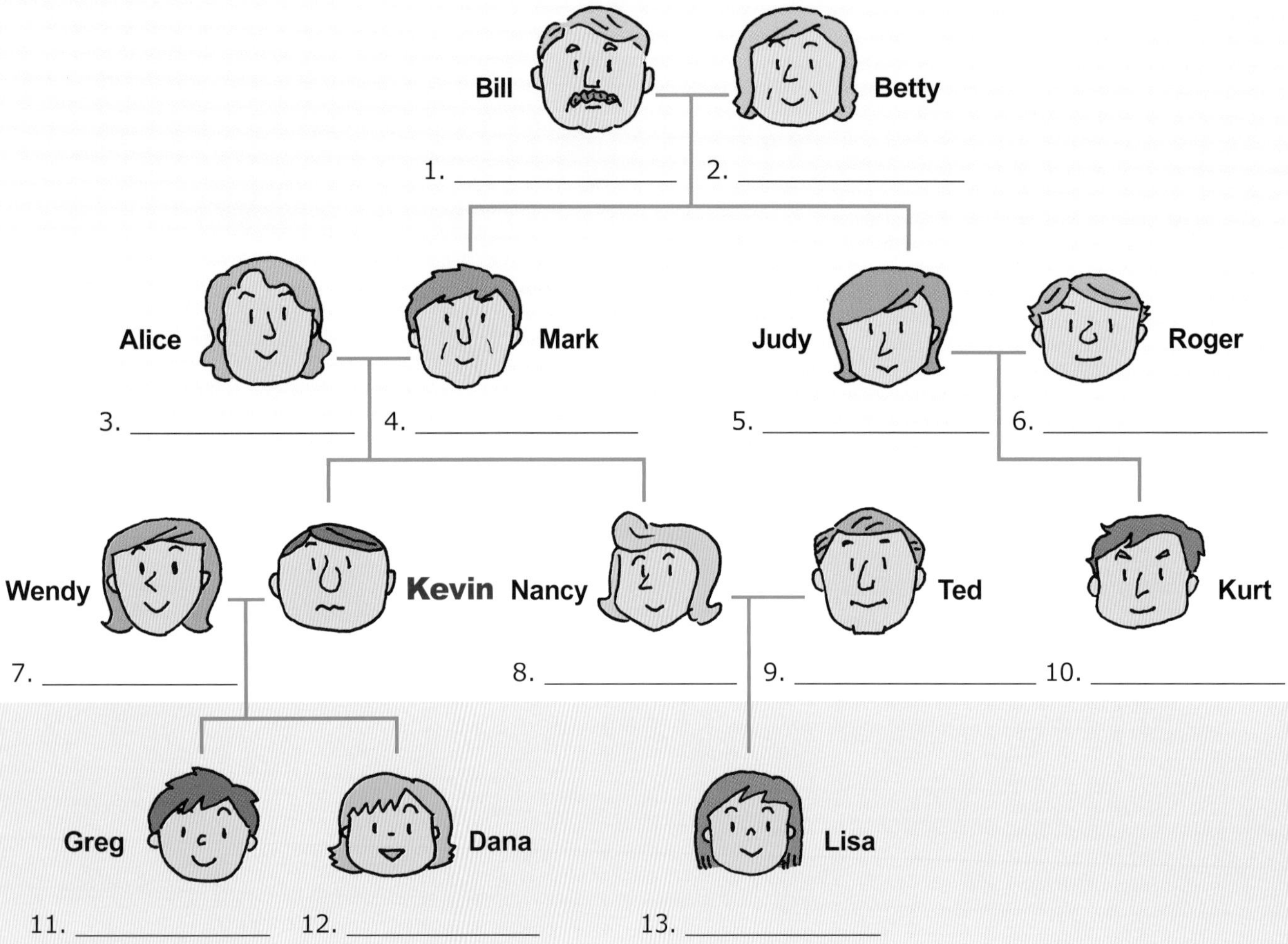

▶Practice 3 Matching: Relatives* 空欄を埋めよう：家族、親戚

Put the correct letters A ～ J in the spaces below.

1 ～ 10 までの空欄に入る最も適切なものを A ～ J から選びましょう。

1. The son of my son is my _____.
2. My mother's sister is my _____.
3. My uncle's son is my _____.
4. The mother of my mother is my _____.
5. My father's daughter is my _____.
6. The man I married is my _____.
7. My brother's son is my _____.
8. My mother's husband is my _____.
9. The brother of my father is my _____.
10. My sister's daughter is my _____.

A. aunt
B. grandmother
C. husband
D. niece
E. uncle
F. grandson
G. sister
H. father
I. cousin
J. nephew

*relatives 親戚

▶Practice 4 Family Words Bingo ファミリーメンバー・ビンゴ

Choose 16 words from the choices below and write them in the bingo card, one word for each box.

以下の語から 16 の単語を選び、ビンゴカードに記入しましょう。順不同でひとつのボックスにひとつの単語を書き入れて下さい。

grandmother grandfather grandparents* grandson
granddaughter grandchildren* sister-in-law brother-in-law
mother-in-law father-in-law stepmother stepfather parents*
children relatives aunt uncle nephew niece cousin

*grandparents 祖父母 grandchildren 孫 parents 両親

Now listen to your teacher describe different family members. You must listen carefully because you won't hear the actual words, but hints that help you guess the words. Cross off the words corresponding to the hints. When you have crossed off four words in a row on your card, shout "Bingo!"

先生が家族 / 親戚について説明します。ヒントをよく聞いて，当てはまる単語があれは消していきます。縦か横一列に 4 つ消すことができたら、大きな声で "Bingo!" と言いましょう。

Bingo Card

▶Practice 5 Family Tree (Part 2) 家系図 パート2

Student A stay on this page. **Student B** turn to **Appendix 6**. There are 15 differences in Trevor's family tree. Ask questions to each other to find the differences.

Student A は以下の絵を見てください。Student B は Appendix 6 を見てください。2 人の見ている Trevor の家系図には 15 か所異なる点があります。お互いに質問しながら違いを見つけましょう。

Examples: What's Steven's last name? What does Trevor do?
How old's Steven's wife? What's Steven's wife's name?

Student A

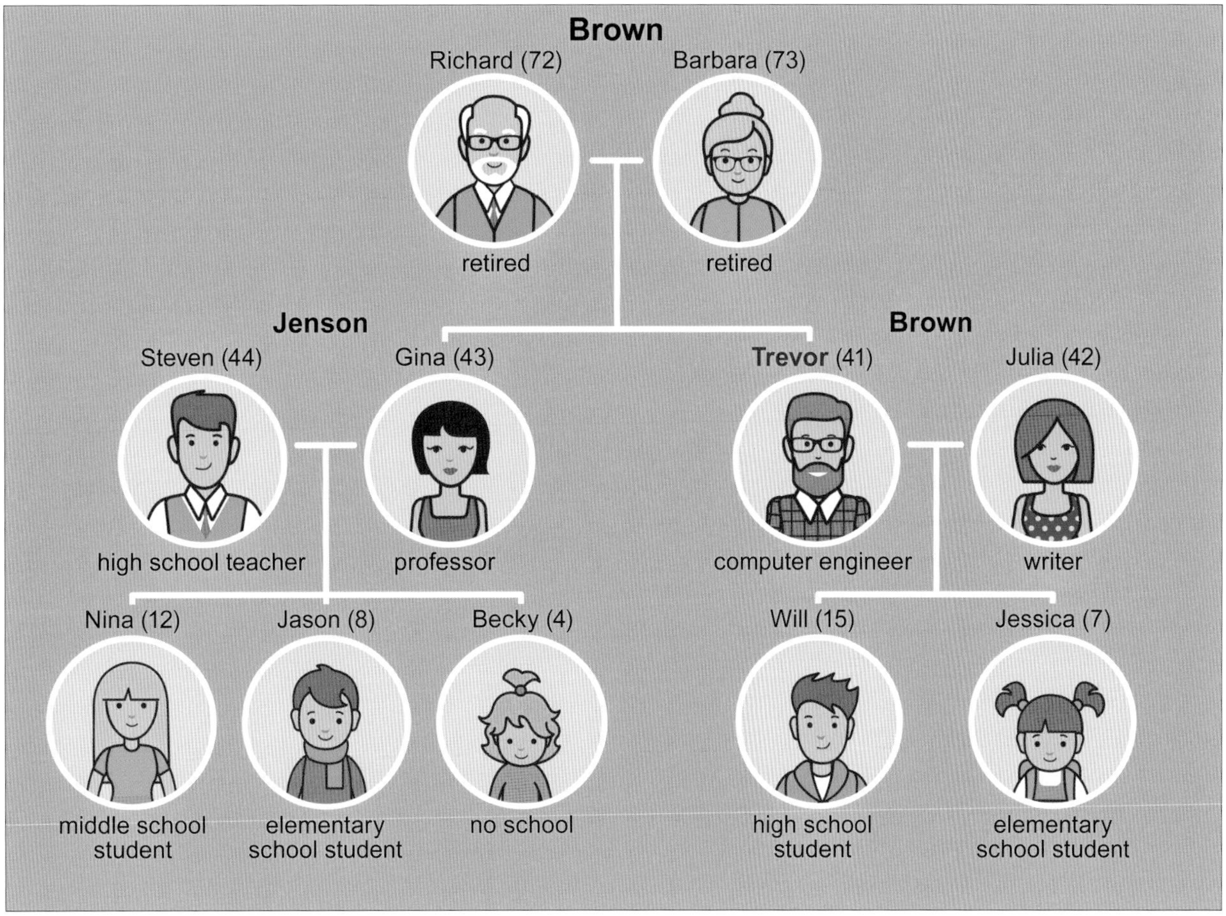

▶Practice 6 Family Tree (Part 3) 家系図 パート3

On a piece of paper, draw your own family tree (like the one in **Practice 2**) on a piece of paper. Then, in groups, take turns introducing your family. Other group members may ask questions.

自分の家系図を書いてみましょう。(Practice 2 を参考に) 書き終わったらグループ内で順番に自分の家族について紹介しましょう。紹介されたらほかのメンバーは、そのクラスメイトの家族について質問してください。

▶Practice 7 Reading リーディング

Parenting Styles*

50

子育てのスタイル

The most important people for babies and children are their parents. There are four kinds of parents. The first type is very strict*. The children must follow family rules* and, if they break the rules*, they are punished*. Children of very strict parents are less* cheerful* and have more stress. The second type of parent has little relationship* or communication with their children and they sometimes neglect* them. Their children often have psychological or social problems* when they grow up*. The third kind of parent is too soft* on their children. They want to be friends with their children, so they do not punish them. Their children are often happy, but some of them become spoiled*. The last kind of parent has a good balance of discipline* and kindness*. They listen to their children and talk to them about many things, including* life experiences* and feelings. Children of these parents learn many important life skills and they are often confident* and responsible*.

* parenting style 子育てスタイル　strict 厳しい　follow rules ルールに従う　break rules ルールを破る　punish 罰する　less ～ あまり～ではない　cheerful 明るい　relationship 関係　neglect ほったらかす、放置する　psychological problem 心理的問題　social problem 社会的問題　grow up 成長する　soft 甘い　spoiled 甘やかされた　discipline 規律　kindness 優しさ　including ～ ～を含む　life experiences 人生経験　confident 自信がある　responsible 責任感のある

True or False 内容把握

Write "T" for true or "F" for false for each of the sentences below.

内容と一致している場合は "T"、一致していなければ "F" を入れましょう。

_____ 1. Friends are more important for babies than parents.

_____ 2. Children with very strict parents are often more negative and have more stress.

_____ 3. Neglected children may have psychological problems when they grow up.

_____ 4. The best kind of parent is one who wants to become friends with their children.

_____ 5. Children who are spoiled develop* important life skills.

_____ 6. Discipline can be good for children.

_____ 7. Children who share their feelings and experiences with parents are usually less confident.

_____ 8. A good parent tries to balance* discipline and kindness.

* develop 発達させる、身につける　balance バランスを取る

▶Practice 8 Group Work: Questions for Discussion グループワーク：話し合ってみよう

1. What kind of parents do you have? Do they have a lot of rules? Do you have a lot of freedom?
2. Do you think parenting styles are changing? If "yes," how are they changing?
3. Do you want to have children? Why or why not?
4. What kind of parent do you want to be? What kind of children do you want?

Grammar 2

51

Modal Verbs: Should, Must, Have to

助動詞：～しなければならない

Children ***should*** help with household chores*.
Students ***shouldn't*** sleep in class.
I ***have to*** do homework this weekend.
Students who are sick ***don't have to*** come to class.
Successful* social workers* ***must*** understand many things about people.
People who take strong medicine* ***mustn't*** drive their car.

*household chore 家事　successful 良好な、成功している　social worker ソーシャルワーカー　medicine 薬

▶Practice 9 Group Work グループワーク

In groups, write down several things that make good parents. Use the modals *should*, *must*, and *have to*, as shown in the grammar examples above.

良い親の条件とは何か考えてみましょう。例文を参考に、should, must, have to を使って文章を書いてみましょう。

Example: Parents should communicate with their children.
Parents must not hit their children.

▶Practice 10 Find Someone Who ... こんな人を探そう

First, complete the questions on the left of the chart below. Then find someone who answers "yes" to the questions and write their names on the right. Talk to as many people as you can.

表の左側の質問を完成させ、それに Yes（否定の質問で聞かれたら答えは No）と答えられる人を見つけ右側の空欄に記入してください。できるだけたくさんの人に聞いてみましょう。

Example: Find someone whose family member has an interesting job.
Question: Does someone in your family have an interesting job?
Answer: Yes, my father's a police officer. (Write down the person's name and write a note like "*Father, police officer.*"

Find Someone ...	**Name**
1. ... who has two sisters or two brothers. Question: ______________________________?	
2. ... whose mother works. Question: ______________________________?	
3. ... who's close to* their cousin. Question: ______________________________?	
4. ... whose grandparent* still works. Question: ______________________________?	
5. ... who has a strict mother or father. Question: ______________________________?	
6. ... who's an only child. Question: ______________________________?	
7. ... who wants a big family. Question: ______________________________?	
8. ... who has a family member with an interesting job. Question: ______________________________?	

*be close to ～に近い、～と仲が良い　grandparent 祖父母（どちらかひとり）

▶Practice 11 Listening リスニング 52

Listen to the following description and write in the missing words below.
文章を聞いて空欄を埋めてください

Hello, everybody. Today, I'd like to describe* __________________. My father's tall and __________________. I'm not sure exactly* how old he is, but __________________ 50's. He likes __________________ very muscular*. My mother's __________________. She's in her late 40's. She has long, thick*, __________________. She has large, dark brown eyes __________________. She doesn't like her nose, but __________________. She __________________. She also likes dancing. She has __________________. My parents are __________________, too. I really respect them.

* describe 説明する　exactly 正確に　muscular 筋肉たくましい　thick hair ふさふさした髪

▶Practice 12 Presentation プレゼンテーション

Now it is time to describe someone you know—a friend, a family member, or another person. Write sentences about their appearance, personality, and any other information you think is important to understand them. After writing your description, practice it so that you can look at your audience when giving your presentation.
さあ、今度はみなさんが友達や家族を紹介する番です。見た目や性格、その他の情報について文を書いてください。書き終わったら、プレゼンテーションをする前に、クラスメイトたちとアイコンタクトをとりながら話せるように練習しましょう。

Unit 8
Communication
コミュニケーション

Speaking

Practice the following dialogues with a partner. After you have practiced the model conversation a few times, substitute the underlined information with the words in the boxes.

以下の会話をパートナーと練習してください。数回練習したら，下線の部分を枠内の表現に言いかえて再度練習しましょう。

Dialogue 1 53

Kumi: What do you do in your free time, Ken?

Ken: Well, I rarely*(1) have free time on weekdays. I work part-time in a restaurant twice a week.*(2) But I spend a lot of time* online* on weekends.

Kumi: Oh, yeah? What do you do online?

Ken: I often(3) watch music videos and text* my friends.

*rarely めったに～ない　twice a week 週に２回　spend time 過ごす
online オンラインで　text（携帯やスマホで）メールする

1. seldom* hardly ever*	2. three times a week every other day*	3. sometimes usually*

*seldom めったに～ない　hardly ever めったに～ない　every other day 一日おきに　usually 普段、通常

Dialogue 2 54

Ken: How about you, Kumi? How often do you go online*?

Kumi: Often,(1) but I hardly ever*(2) play computer games.

Ken: What about* TV? Do you watch TV often?

Kumi: I seldom(3) watch TV. I prefer* checking my smartphone. My parents tell me I'm addicted* to it!

*go online インターネット通信を使う　hardly ever めったに～ない　What about ～ ～はどうですか?
prefer ～ ～の方が好き　addicted to ～ ～の中毒になる

1. sometimes occasionally*	2. rarely never	3. hardly ever rarely

*occasionally ときどき

Grammar 1

55

Adverbs of Frequency

頻度を表す副詞

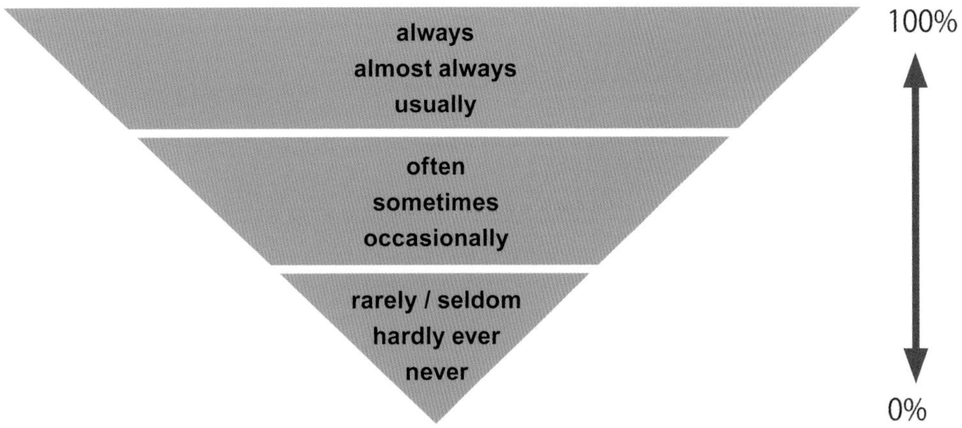

Other Expressions of Frequency

once a day
twice a week
three times a month
every morning
every other day

▶Practice 1 Grammar Exercise どのくらい頻繁にしていますか？

Write answers that are true for you.

自分のことについて答えてみましょう。

Example: How ***often*** do you watch TV?
I watch TV every day.

How ***long*** do you ***spend*** online each day?
I spend about 80 minutes online on average.*

*on average 平均で

1. How often do you go online?

____

2. How often do you text your friends?

____

3. How often do you read newspapers?

____

4. How long do you study every day on average?

____

5. How often do you play computer games?

____

6. How long do you spend online every day?

____

7. How often do you read comic books*?

____

8. How long do you spend texting your friends every day?

____

* comic books マンガ

Pair work: Now ask these questions to a partner.

▶Practice 2 Listening リスニング 56

Listen to the passage and write in the missing words.

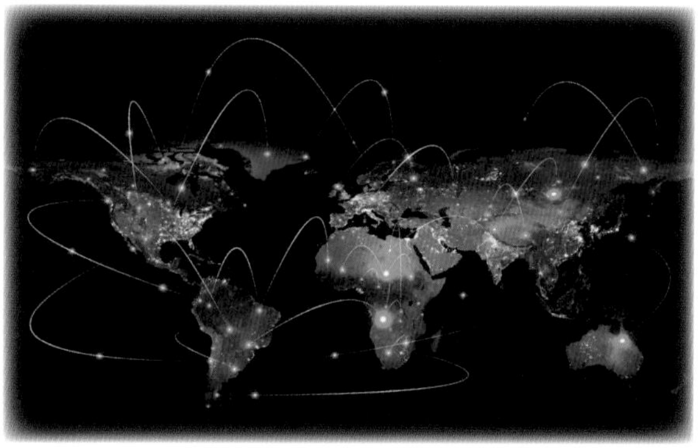

The world today is a ____________________ than it was a hundred years ago. We can ______________________ easily and quickly. We communicate with people ________________________ by technology. Many people do ________ ______________. People ________________ foreign countries and ________________. These ________________ globalization, and they ________________. However, ________________ communication and even life more complicated*. Because of cultural differences*, we ________________ when we communicate with foreigners*, but we can ________________ our mistakes.

* complicated 複雑な cultural difference 文化的な違い foreigner 外国人

▶Practice 3 Matching: Ways to Communicate 絵に合うものをさがそう：コミュニケーションの方法

Put the words in the box under the correct picture.

絵を表す単語を枠内から選びましょう。

telephone　art　smartphone　gesture*　newspaper　book
social networking site (SNS)　radio　television　letter　email

*gesture ジェスチャー

A. ____________________

B. ____________________

C. ____________________

D. ____________________

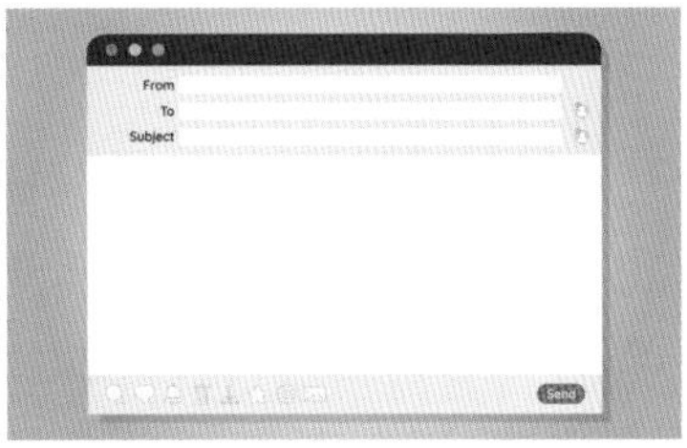

E. ____________________

F. ____________________

G. ____________________

H. ____________________

I. ____________________

J. ____________________

K. ____________________

▶Practice 4 Reading: Communication リーディング：コミュニケーション

57

Humans are very good at communication. Many animals communicate, too, but humans can communicate much better.

When we hear the word "communication," we often think of people talking to each other. But humans communicate in many different ways. We use words and grammar to talk, but we use more than just words. We use such things as intonation, voice loudness, stress, and speed. We also communicate with our bodies, such as gestures and expressions on our faces. These types of body language are called "nonverbal communication."

There are about 6,000 languages in the world today. Language lets us do many things, like sharing our thoughts, opinions, and feelings. We can make new friends, do business, tell jokes, write stories, tell lies, share secrets, and get people to do the things we want them to do. We can also talk about the past and future, something animals cannot do. In addition to speaking and listening, humans can read and write. Writing lets us share knowledge. It also lets us communicate with people in the future.

Communication has changed a lot recently. Technology is changing the way we communicate. We send email, text, share messages on social networking sites, and do much more. We get information as well as entertainment from the different kinds of media, including computers, TV, and movies. Our ancestors would be shocked to see the different ways we communicate today. Just imagine what your great grandfather would think if he could see you on your computer or smartphone.

* communicate コミュニケーションをとる　each other お互いに　grammar 文法
intonation イントネーション　loudness（音の）大きさ　stress 強勢、アクセント
expression 表現　nonverbal 非言語　thought 考え　opinion 意見
tell lies うそをつく　past 過去　future 未来　in addition to ～ ～に加えて
let ～させる、してくれる　knowledge 知識　recently 最近
entertainment エンタテイメント、娯楽芸能　ancestors 祖先
imagine 想像する　great grandfather ひいおじいさん

True or False 内容把握

Read the following sentences. Write T if the sentence is true and F if the sentence is false.

以下の文章が内容と合っていれば “T”、合っていなければ “F” を空欄に入れましょう。

____ 1. When people speak to each other, they use only words and grammar.

____ 2. Nonverbal communication is communication without words.

____ 3. Facial expressions* are a kind of nonverbal communication.

____ 4. Animals can communicate about the past and future.

____ 5. Writing lets us communicate to people in the future.

____ 6. Technology has changed how we communicate today.

* facial expression 表情

▶Practice 5 Find Someone Who … こんな人を探そう

Find someone who answers “yes” to the survey questions. Then ask an additional question. Write notes in “**Extra Information**.”

表の左側の質問を完成させ、それに Yes（否定の質問で聞かれたら答えは No）と答えられる人を見つけ右側の空欄に記入してください。もうひとつ質問してその答えを “Extra Information” に書きましょう。

Example: A: Do you text more than* one hour a day?
B: Yes, I do.
A: Who do you text?
B: Usually my friends, but I sometimes text my mother when I come home late.

* more than ～ ～以上

Find Someone Who …	Name	Extra Information
1. … texts more than one hour a day on average.		
2. … looks at their smartphone in class.		
3. … talks to their pet.		
4. … sometimes communicates to others* in English.		
5. … watches TV more than two hours a day on average.		

Find Someone Who ...	Name	Extra Information
6. ... loves reading books.		
7. ... knows someone without a smartphone.		
8. ... plays computer games more than an hour a day on average.		
9. ... made a friend through the internet.*		
10. ... likes face-to-face* conversation more than texting.		

* others ほかの（人たち）　through the internet インターネットを通して　face-to-face 対面で、顔を見て

▶Practice 6 Group Work: Communication グループワーク：コミュニケーション

Discuss the following questions together in groups.

以下の質問についてグループで話し合ってみましょう。

1. How is communication changing?
2. In what ways do you communicate every day?
3. What new words do young people use today?
4. Do Japanese use a lot of gestures compared to* people in other cultures? What kind of gestures do you use?
5. Do you think nonverbal* communication in Japan is changing? If yes, how is it changing?
6. What are some sounds or noises* that Japanese make to communicate something?

* compared to ～ ～と比べると　nonverbal 非言語の　noises 音

▶Practice 7 Text Messaging (1) 携帯でメッセージ（1）

Text messages often have their own form of spelling and grammar.

携帯を使ったメールでは、特別な省略形やスペルを使うことがあります。

Examples: 'u' which means 'you'
'cu' which means 'see you'
'oc' which means 'of course'

Match the text message on the left with the standard English on the right.
1～15のメッセージの意味を、A～Oまでのメッセージから選びましょう。

______ 1. *b4*	A. to you
______ 2. *ily*	B. Are you OK?
______ 3. *2u*	C. before
______ 4. *thx*	D. Got to go.
______ 5. *bc*	E. Sorry.
______ 6. *ur*	F. by the way
______ 7. *tho*	G. because
______ 8. *ttyl*	H. Thanks.
______ 9. *bff*	I. Great.
______ 10. *gtg*	J. I love you.
______ 11. *ruok*	K. Talk to you later.
______ 12. *ik*	L. your / you're
______ 13. *btw*	M. though
______ 14. *sry*	N. best friends forever
______ 15. *gr8*	O. I know.

▶Practice 8 Text Messaging (2) 携帯でメッセージ (2)

Change the following text messages into standard English.
次のメッセージを普通の英文に直しましょう。想像力を使ってください。

Examples: *c u later* See you later.
where ru? Where are you?

1. *how ru?* ______________________________
2. *its 4u* ______________________________
3. *i want 2go* ______________________________
4. *cu 2morrow* ______________________________
5. *ur gr8!* ______________________________
6. *do u want 2c a movie 2morrow?* ______________________________

▶Practice 9 Nonverbal Communication 非言語コミュニケーション

Match the communication expressed in the pictures by putting the correct letter next to the sentences below.

以下の絵は何を伝えようとしているのでしょうか？ 1 ～ 16 の英語表現を表す絵を A ～ P の中から選んでください。

A.

B.

C.

D.

E.

F.

G.

H.

I.

J.

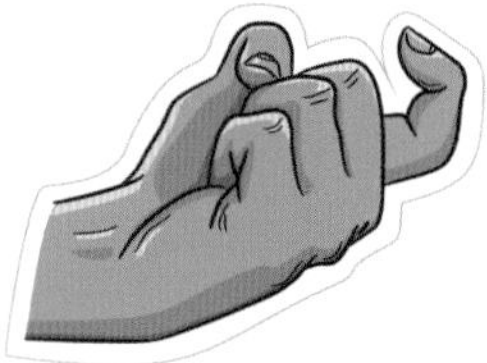

K.

L.

M.

N.

O.

P.

______ 1. Do you want to fight?
______ 2. I'm in a hurry!
______ 3. Go away!
______ 4. I'm tired.
______ 5. Stop!
______ 6. I'm so sorry.
______ 7. It stinks.
______ 8. I love you.
______ 9. I don't know.
______ 10. I'm scared.
______ 11. Come here.
______ 12. I'm depressed.*
______ 13. Yuck!*
______ 14. It's hot.
______ 15. Yay!
______ 16. Good job!*

*depressed 落ち込んだ　yuck! ゲー！　stink 臭い　good job! よくやったね！

▶Practice 10 Mime Activity ジェスチャーゲーム

Your teacher will give you some words for you to act out nonverbally. Try your best and have fun!

感情を表す表現を、言葉を使わずに体や表情を使って表してみましょう。楽しみながらゲーム感覚でやってみましょう。

Unit 9

How Are You Feeling?

どんな気分？

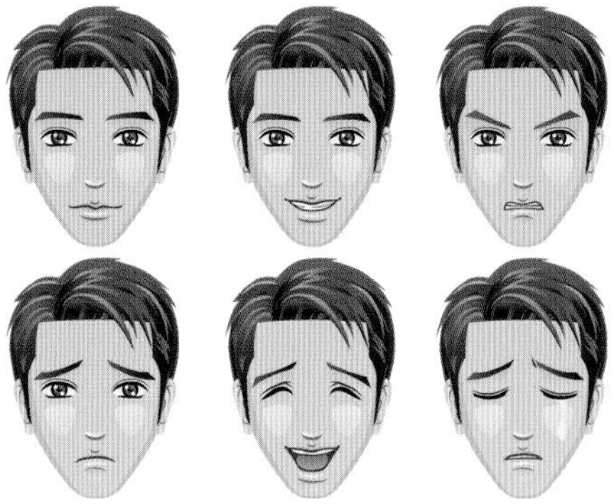

Matching: Feeling Words

Put the "feeling words" in the box under the correct picture.

それぞれの絵がどんな感情を表しているかを枠内から選びましょう。

disappointed*　jealous*　frustrated*　bored*　confused*　angry*
ashamed*　proud*　scared*　excited*　shocked*　relaxed*
embarrassed*

1. ______________________

2. ______________________

3. ______________________

4. ______________________

5. ______________________

6. ______________________

7. ______________________

8. ______________________

9. ______________________

10. ______________________

11. ______________________

12. ______________________

13. ______________________

*disappointed　がっかりする　jealous　うらやましがる　frustrated　いらいらする
bored　つまらなく感じる　confused　混乱する　angry　怒っている　ashamed　恥じる
proud　誇りに思う　scared　怖がる　excited　わくわくする　shocked　びっくりする
relaxed　リラックスする　embarrassed　恥ずかしいと感じる

Note: **Ashamed, Embarrassed, and Shy の違い**

Ashamed, embarrassed, and shy are all different:

Ashamed　A feeling when you do something bad or wrong and feel guilty* about it.
社会的通念や、道徳的に悪いことをしたときに罪の意識を感じる。

Embarrassed　A feeling when you make a stupid mistake and are afraid other people will laugh at you.
おかしなミスをした時など、他人に対して恥ずかしいと感じる。

Shy　A feeling when it's difficult for you to be open to other people.
恥ずかしがりや、人見知り

*guilty　罪の意識を感じる

Speaking

Practice the following dialogues with a partner. After you have practiced the model conversation a few times, substitute the underlined information with the words in the boxes.

以下の会話をパートナーと練習してください。数回練習したら，下線の部分を枠内の表現に言いかえて再度練習しましょう。

Dialogue 1　58

Anna: Is everything OK, Pedro? You look kind of* nervous.*(1)

Pedro: Yeah, I am.

Anna: How come?*(2)

Pedro: I have a job interview*(3) tomorrow.

Anna: Oh, really? Well, good luck. I'm sure* it will go well.*

Pedro: Yeah, I hope so.*

1. excited worried	2. Why's that? Why?	3. date big test

*kind of　何だか　nervous　緊張する　how come?　なぜ？　job interview　面接
I'm sure ～　絶対～だと思う　go well　うまくいく　I hope so.　そうだといいな

Dialogue 2 59

Emi: Hi, David. What's up? You look really happy!(1)

David: I just got some good news.

Emi: Oh, yeah?

David: I was offered* a job.(2)

Emi: Oh, really?

David: I can't believe it. I'm so excited.(3)

Emi: Wow! That's really exciting!(4) I'm happy to hear that, David.

David: Thanks, Emi.

1. pleased* thrilled*	2. was admitted* to Harvard got engaged*	3. thrilled happy	4. wonderful amazing*

*be offered a job 仕事が決まった　pleased うれしい　thrilled わくわくする
admitted 入学を許可される　get engaged 婚約する　amazing すばらしい

Dialogue 3 60

Richard: You seem* kind of down* today, Stella. Are you OK?

Stella: Umm... I just got some bad news.

Richard: Oh, yeah? What is it?

Stella: My parents are getting divorced*.(1)

Richard: Wow. That's too bad*.(2)

Stella: I just can't believe it. I'm so depressed*.(3)

Richard: That really is depressing.*(4) I'm sorry* to hear that, Stella.

1. dog died dad is in the hospital	2. terrible* a shame*	3. upset* worried	4. upsetting worrying

*seem～ ～に見える　down 落ち込んでいる　get divorced 離婚する　too bad お気の毒に
depressed 落ち込んでいる　I'm sorry お気の毒です　terrible ひどい
That's a shame. それは残念です　upset 動揺する

Grammar 1

61

Asking About and Expressing Feelings

相手の気持ちを聞く、自分の感情を表す

Questions:	**Answers:**
How are you feeling / doing today?	I'm a little depressed. / I'm great.
Are you angry?	Yes, I am. / No, I'm not.
Why are you looking so happy?	I just got an A on my test.
How come you look so pleased today?	I have a new boyfriend.
What's wrong?	I failed the test.
What's the matter?	To tell the truth, I'm really nervous.
Are you OK?	Not really. I'm feeling down.
Is everything alright?	Yeah, I'm fine.
You look kind of down. Are you OK?	I just got some bad news.

▶Practice 1 How Are You Feeling?

Choose the correct words from the box below to complete the sentences. More than one answer may be possible.

感情を表す最も適切な表現を枠内から選んで文章を完成させましょう。

scared 怖がる　excited わくわくする　nervous 緊張する　worried 心配する
depressed 落ち込む　interested 興味がある　bored つまらない
disappointed がっかりする　embarrassed はずかしい　confused 混乱する
relieved 安心する　relaxed リラックスする

1. **Yu:** How was your trip to Hakone, Mike?
   Mike: It was great. Our hotel had an *onsen*, so now I feel very ________________.
2. **Roger:** What's the matter? You don't look happy.
   Yuichi: This class is too easy for me. I'm ________________.
3. **Jun:** What are you reading?
   Pipa: A book about Mother Theresa. I'm ________________ in her life story, so I borrowed* it from the library.
4. **Miyu:** Is everything OK?
   Mari: No, not really. I walked into the men's restroom by mistake. I was so ________________.

*borrow 借りる

5. **Paul:** Did you win the game?

Mai: No, we lost. I'm a little ________________.

6. **Sue:** How come you look so happy today?

Hana: I'm going to see my favorite band in concert tonight, and I'm feeling really ________________.

7. **Blake:** What's wrong?

Stephanie: My son has a really high fever*. I'm so ________________ about him.

8. **Marge:** Why were you late for class today?

Mai: I was ________________ at the station and got on the wrong* train.

9. **Kei:** What's the matter?

Naoyuki: I asked my girlfriend to marry me, but she said "no". I'm so ______________.

10. **Naomi:** Why are you looking so pleased?

Carl: I got 100% on my test today. I didn't study for it and I thought I'd get a really low score, so I'm really ________________.

11. **Jo:** How was the movie?

Sue: It was a horror movie. I was so ________________.

12. **Jan:** Are you looking forward to going to England?

Mark: To be honest, I hate flying, so I'm really ________________ about the trip.

*fever 熱　wrong 間違った

Grammar 2

62

Adjectives with -ed and -ing

現在分詞や過去分詞を形容詞として使う

When we talk about our own or another person's feelings, we often use adjectives that end in "ed", such as "I'm surprised." In other words, we use the "ed" ending when the feeling is inside us. When we talk about an outside event that gives us a feeling, we often use an "ing" ending, such as "The news is surprising."

感情を表すときに、現在分詞（動詞の～ing 形）や過去分詞（動詞の過去分詞形 ～ed など）を形容詞として使うことがあります。自分の感情を表すときは、過去分詞（I'm surprised. など）を使い、「何かが、自分にある感情を起こさせる」場合や、ある事象の説明をするときは、現在分詞（The news is surprising など）を使います。

I am ～ ed. He/She is ～ ed. We/They are ～ ed.（過去分詞を形容詞のように使う）

interested, shocked, excited, bored, disappointed, embarrassed, surprised, frustrated*, confused, moved, relaxed

It is ～ ing.（現在分詞を形容詞のように使う）

interesting, shocking, exciting, boring, disappointing, embarrassing, surprising, frustrating*, confusing, moving*, relaxing

* frustrated / frustrating　いらいらする　　moved / moving　感動する

▶Practice 2 How Does it Make You Feel? どんな気持ちになる？

Look back at your answers to **Practice 1**. Most speakers used the '~ed' pattern to explain their feelings. Now use the '~ing' pattern to explain how the outside event made each person feel.

Practice 1 ではすべて過去分詞（～ ed）を使って感情を表しました。今度は、現在分詞（～ ing）を使って気持ちを表してみましょう。

1. How was Mike's trip to Hakone?

   It was ______________________________.

2. How's Yuichi's class?

   It's ______________________________.

3. How's Mother Teresa's life story?

   It's ______________________________.

4. How did Mari feel about her mistake?

   It was ______________________________.

5. How was the game?

   It was ______________________________.

6. How does Hana feel about the concert?

   It's ______________________________.

7. How does Stephanie feel about her son's fever?

   It's ______________________________.

8. Why was Mai late?

   Because the station was ______________________________.

9. What's the matter with Naoyuki?

   His girlfriend's answer was ______________________________.

▶Practice 3 Feeling Words 感情を表す表現

Choose the correct words from the box to complete the sentences below.

枠内から、それぞれの絵を表す感情表現を選んで空欄に入れましょう。

disappointed confusing disappointing surprising scared bored
irritating* surprised irritated* boring scary confused

* irritated / irritating いらいらする

1. I'm very ______________________.

2. The movie was very ______________.

3. This software is so ______________.

4. I'm so ________________________.

5. He was ________________________.

6. The news was ______________.

7. They're ________________________.

8. The class is ______________________.

9. The mosquitoes* are ______________.

10. I'm ______________ by the mosquitoes.

11. My grade* is very ________________.

12. She's very __________________ with her son's grade.

* mosquito 蚊　　grade 成績

Grammar 3

63

Yes and No Questions

否定の疑問文や付加疑問文で聞かれた時の Yes/No の答え方

～でしょう？、～だよね？

The answers to negative questions differ in English and in Japanese.

否定疑問文で聞かれた時の答えは日本語と英語では異なります。

In English 英語で答えるとき

Q: Aren't you happy?　　あなたは幸せじゃないの？
You aren't happy, are you?　　あなたは幸せじゃないよね？

A: Yes, I am.　　うん、幸せだよ。
No, I'm not.　　ううん（いいえ）幸せじゃない。

In Japanese 日本語で答えるとき

Q: あなたは幸せじゃないの？
あなたは幸せじゃないよね？

A: うん、幸せじゃない。
ううん（いいえ）幸せだよ。

▶Practice 4 Pair Work: Yes / No Questions ペアワーク：Yes/No の質問

Take turns asking and answering the following questions.

パートナーと順番に質問し合いましょう。

1. The little girl is happy, isn't she?

2. Isn't he shocked?

3. Is he nervous?

4. He's excited, isn't he?

5. Isn't the class interesting?

▶Practice 5 Reading: Emotions* リーディング：感情

64

We all have emotions, but we show them and share them in different ways. Some people are very open with their feelings, while some people share them only with close friends* or family members. These differences are caused* by differences in personality, in experience*, and in culture*. Americans, for example, often show feelings more openly* than Japanese. Children often show their emotions freely*, but most of us learn to control our emotions as* we grow up.

Our emotions are affected* by our values*. We feel that certain behaviors* are right* and other behaviors are wrong*, some things are good and other things bad. Some people think all humans are the same and have the same values, but this is not true. We all have different values. We learn them from our parents, from school, from friends, and from the media. Many of our values are cultural*.

*emotion 感情　close friend 親しい友人　cause 起こす　experience 経験　culture 文化
openly オープンに　freely 自由に　as 〜につれて　affect 影響する　value 価値観
behaviour 行動、振る舞い　right 正しい　wrong 間違った　cultural 文化的な

True or False 内容把握

Write "T" for true or "F" for false for each of the sentences below.

内容と一致している場合は "T"、一致していなければ "F" を入れましょう。

_____ 1. Almost all* people show their feelings openly.

_____ 2. Americans usually show their feelings more openly than Japanese.

_____ 3. Children and adults* usually show their feelings equally*.

_____ 4. Our values affect our emotions.

_____ 5. Humans share most of the important values.

_____ 6. We learn our values from different people around us*.

* almost all ほとんど全ての　adult 大人　equally 同じように　people around us 私たちの周りの人たち

►Practice 6 Group Discussion: Culture and Emotions グループディスカッション：文化と感情

Look at the pictures below and discuss. How do the foreigners visiting Japan feel? Why?

以下の絵を見てクラスメイトと話し合ってください。日本を訪れている外国人はどう感じるでしょう？また、なぜそう感じるのでしょうか？

1.

2.

3.

4.

▶Practice 7 Your Emotions 自分の気持ち

Rate each of the situations, writing '1' for the situation that gives you the strongest emotion, '2' for the second strongest emotion, etc.

以下の状況に対してどう感じるか、自分の気持ちが強いものから弱いものまで順番を付けましょう。最も強く感じる場合は 1、それより弱いものには 2 を付けてください。

1. What makes you the angriest?

☐ 

A. A person with a smart phone blocks* your way.

☐ 

B. A young person takes an old person's train seat.

☐ 

C. A person talks on a smart phone loudly*.

☐ 

D. Someone cuts in line* in front of you.

☐ 

E. Someone borrows* money and doesn't pay it back*.

2. What makes you the happiest?

☐ 

A. A surprise birthday gift from a friend.

☐ 

B. You win* a competition*.

☐ 

C. You get the highest score on a test.

☐ 

D. You get your dream job.

☐ 

E. You meet your favorite star.

* block 阻む　loudly 大きな声で　cut in line 割り込む　borrow 借りる
pay back (お金を)返す　win 勝つ　competition 試合

3. What scares* you the most?

A. snakes

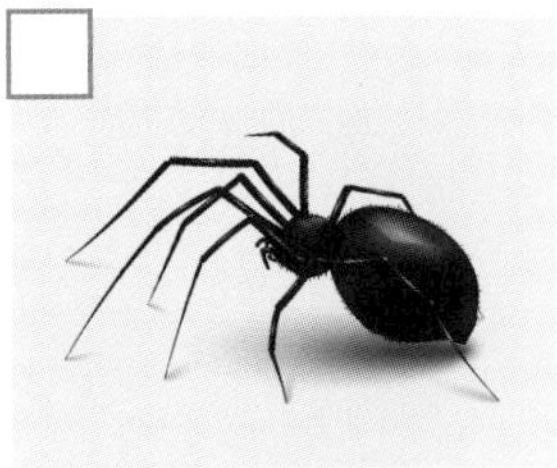

B. spiders

C. ghosts

D. scary clowns*

E. heights*

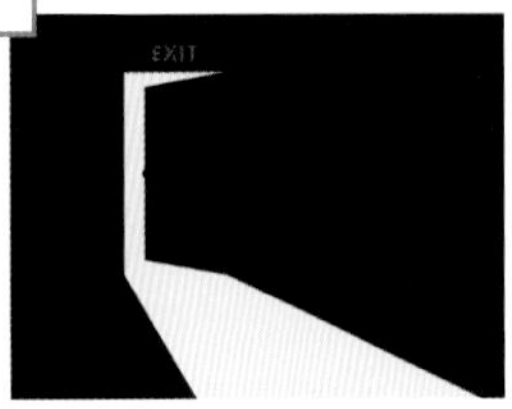

F. the dark

G. tests

H. flying

* scare 怖がらせる　clown ピエロ　heights 高さ

▶Practice 8 Listening リスニング 65

Listen to the dialogue and write in the missing words.

会話を聞いて空欄を埋めましょう。

Dana: Is everything OK, Eri? You ______________________________.

Eri: Well, ______________. I ______________________________.

Dana: Really? Aren't you doing well?

Eri: No, I'm not. I ______________________, but I ______________

______________ English. I'm frustrated*.

Dana: Well, ______________________ can be ______________, but you have to take it step by step. You can be more patient*, ______________?

Eri: Well, __________, I __________.

* frustrated いらいらする　patient がまん強い

▶Practice 9 Group Work: Gesture Game グループワーク：ジェスチャーゲーム

Your teacher will give you feeling words to act out in groups. Try to get other students to guess the word. Use gestures and facial expressions only.

グループを作り、一人がジェスチャーで気持ちを表します。ほかのメンバーはクラスメイトの気持ちを英語であてます。表情とジェスチャーのみで気持ちを表してください。以下の表現を使って練習しましょう。

Example: A: (Use gestures or expressions on your face to describe "angry.")
B: Are you sad?
A: No, I'm not sad.
C: Are you angry?
A: Yes, I'm angry!

▶Practice 10 Pair Work ペアワーク

Part 1

Complete the sentences below, describing when you feel the emotions.

次の感情を感じるときはどんなときですか？文章を完成させましょう。

1. I feel happy when ______________________________.
2. I get upset* when ______________________________.
3. I feel sad when ______________________________.
4. I get excited when ______________________________.
5. I feel embarrassed when ______________________________.
6. I feel bad when ______________________________.
7. I freak out* (panic) when ______________________________.
8. I get envious* when ______________________________.

*get upset 怒る、動揺する　freak out パニックする　envious うらやましがる

Part 2

Now, work in pairs. Take turns asking questions about the eight emotions above. For answers, use the structure, "When + S + V."

上記の 8 つの感情について、パートナーと順番に質問しあいましょう。答えるときは "When + S + V" の形を使いましょう。

Example: A: When do you feel excited?
B: I feel excited when I go to a concert.

▶Practice 1 Crossword クロスワード

Work in pairs.. **Student A**: Look at this page. **Student B**: Turn to **Appendix 7**. Give hints to help your partner guess the words that you can see in your half of the crossword. But do not say the actual words in your hints. Then listen to your partner and write in the words that he / she is describing.

ペアになって，Student A はこのページを，Student B は Appendix 7 を見てください。それぞれのクロスワードですでに埋まっている単語をパートナーに当ててもらいます。ヒントを出し合い，お互いのクロスワードの空欄を埋めましょう。 答えを言ってしまわないように気を付けて。

Example:
B: What's "4 across"?
A: This is something you send online to friends and family.
B: Pictures? Email?
A: No, these are often just a few words. Text…
B: Message!
A: Yes, that's it!

Student A

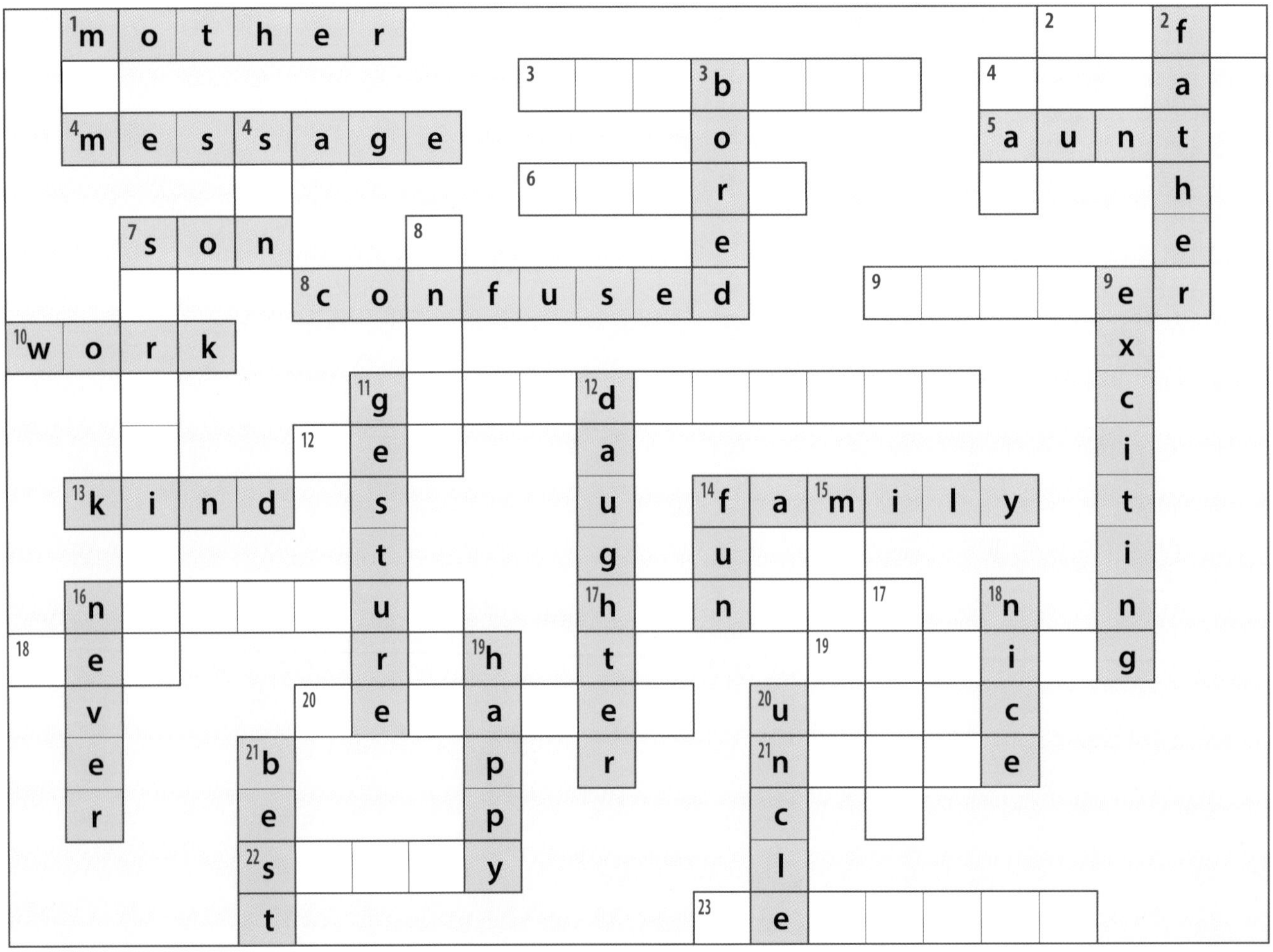

▶Practice 2 Listening: Touch リスニング：スキンシップ 66

Listen to the passage and write in the missing words.

英文を聞いて空欄を埋めましょう。

Touch is an ________________________ communication and often communicates feeling. We ______________________________ when we want to show warmth* (for example, a hug* or pat on the back*) or love (for example, ______________________ __________). Japan is considered* a noncontact* culture, where adults* do not often touch ________________ in public*—especially adults of the opposite sex*. For example, the Japanese bow* is ________________ nonverbal greeting* without touching. It replaces* the handshake*, which is common* ______________________________. However, ____________________ a lot of touching ______________________ ______ (the Japanese-English word "skinship" shows this).

* warmth 暖かさ hug 抱きしめること pat on the back 背中を軽くたたく considered みなされる noncontact 非接触の adult 大人 in public 公の場で opposite sex 異性 bow おじぎ nonverbal greeting 非言語の挨拶 replace ～に取ってかわる handshake 握手 common 一般的な

Unit 10
Memories
思い出

Speaking

Practice the following dialogues with a partner. After you have practiced the model conversation a few times, substitute the underlined information with the words in the boxes.

以下の会話をパートナーと練習してください。数回練習したら，下線の部分を枠内の表現に言いかえて再度練習しましょう。

Dialogue 1 67

Granddaughter: What are you doing, grandma?

Grandmother: I'm looking through* an old photo album I found in the drawer*.

Granddaughter: Oh, really? What's that one?

Grandmother: It's a picture of my honeymoon.*(1)

Granddaughter: Oh, wow! Where did you go?(2)

Grandmother: We went to Hawaii.(3)

Granddaughter: You look so happy.

Grandmother: Yes, it was a happy time.

1. graduation* dog	2. What did you study? What was his name?	2. I studied history. He was called Sammy.

*look through 目を通す　drawer 引き出し　honeymoon 新婚旅行　graduation 卒業（する）

Dialogue 2 68

Stuart: What's your happiest memory, Mina?

Mina: Well, I guess* it was my 18th birthday. My friends planned(1) a party for me and I was so surprised.(2) How about you?

Stuart: My best experience was yesterday. Don't tell anyone,(3) but I just got engaged.*

Mina: Really? When are you getting married*?

Stuart: Sometime next fall.

1. organized	2. it was a real surprise	3. It's a secret

*I guess ～だと思う、～かな　get engaged 婚約する　get married 結婚する

Dialogue 3 69

Robert: What's your earliest* memory, Gina?

Gina: Well, I guess it was when my mom read me a book at bedtime.*(1)

Robert: What book did she read?(2)

Gina: I can't remember exactly.* I think it was a fairy tale.*(3)

Robert: How old were you?

Gina: I was only about three years old. And what's your earliest memory, Robert?

Robert: My fourth birthday* party. My mother made a special cake for me.

1. dad took* me to the park	2. What did you do there	3. we played catch*

*earliest 最も昔の　bedtime 寝る時間　exactly 正確に　fairy tale おとぎ話
fourth birthday 4歳の誕生日　take 連れて行く　play catch キャッチボールをする

Grammar 1 70

Past Tense

過去形

What **did** you do last weekend?	I **went** shopping with my friends.
Did you go anywhere on your last vacation?	Yes, in the summer I **went** to Europe with my family.
How **was** the weather on your trip?	It **was** cloudy most days.
Did you do your homework?	Oh, no! I **forgot**.
How **did** you get an "A" on the test?	I **studied** very hard.

▶Practice 1 Grammar: Simple Past of Irregular Verbs (1) 不規則変化の動詞の過去形 (1)

Write the simple past of the following verbs. The first one has been done for you.

以下の過去形を書いてください。

Verb	Simple Past	Verb	Simple Past
1. begin	*began*	10. hear	____________
2. bring	____________	11. leave	____________
3. buy	____________	12. run	____________
4. come	____________	13. sit	____________
5. drink	____________	14. sleep	____________
6. eat	____________	15. spend	____________
7. fall	____________	16. stand	____________
8. get	____________	17. wake	____________
9. go	____________	18. write	____________

▶Practice 2 Grammar: Simple Past of Irregular Verbs (2) 不規則変化の動詞の過去形 (2)

Change the sentences to the simple past.

以下の文章を過去形に変えてください。

Example:

Momo sings in the shower every day.
Momo sang in the shower yesterday.

1. I go to the station every weekday.
   I ____________ to the station 30 minutes ago.

2. The class begins at 9 a.m. every day.
   The class ____________ at 9 a.m. yesterday.

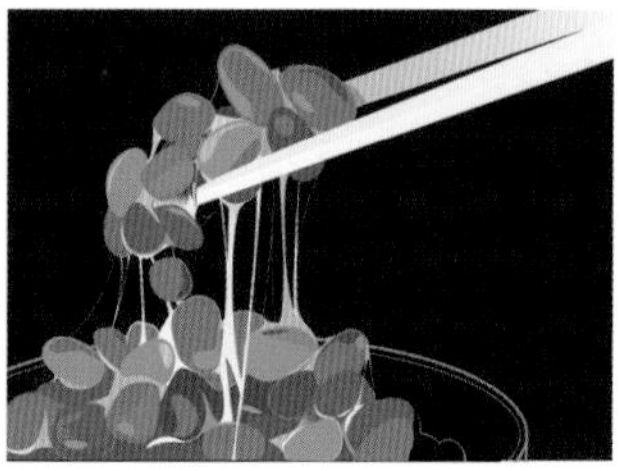

3. Nanami eats *natto* every morning.
   Nanami ____________ *natto* this morning.

4. Yayoi drinks green tea every day.
   Yayoi ____________ green tea yesterday.

5. Kate sees her boyfriend most weekends.
   Kate ____________ her boyfriend last weekend.

6. I speak with my sister often.
   I ____________ with my sister an hour ago.

7. Nao brings a *bento* to school most days.
   Nao ____________ a *bento* to school yesterday.

8. We often hear that song on the radio.
   We just ____________ that song on the radio again.

9. Masa usually leaves the office at 7 p.m.
   Masa ____________ the office at 7 p.m. yesterday.

10. I buy a cup of coffee every morning.
    I ____________ a cup of coffee yesterday.

11. Tom sleeps in a lot of classes.
    Tom ____________ in class this morning.

12. Peter usually stands on the train while* going to work.
    Peter ____________ on the train this morning.

13. I spend a lot of money when shopping.
    I ____________ a lot of money yesterday.

14. Natasha writes in her diary every night.
    Natasha ____________ in her diary ten minutes ago.

*while～ ～の間

▶Practice 3 Writing: Simple Past

Write answers to the following questions using full sentences.

以下の質問に、主語、動詞を入れた文で答えてください。

Example: A: What did you do on your last birthday?
B: I had a birthday party with my family.

1. What did you do last weekend? ______________________________
2. Where did you go on your last vacation? ______________________________
3. What did you eat for breakfast this morning? ______________________________
4. Where did you go after class yesterday? ______________________________
5. Who did you sit next to in class yesterday? ______________________________
6. Where did you leave this book last night? ______________________________
7. What did you bring to class today? ______________________________
8. What time did English class begin today? ______________________________
9. What did you last buy at a convenience store*? ______________________________
10. How much did it cost*? ______________________________
11. How much money did you spend yesterday? ______________________________

Now ask the questions to your partner.

* convenience store コンビニ cost（お金などが）かかる

▶Practice 4 Pair Work: Running Dictation ストーリー

You are now going to do a running dictation. Listen carefully to your teacher's instructions and have fun in this contest. Good luck!

ストーリーをつくるゲームをします。先生の説明をよく聞いてゲームを楽しみましょう。

Key Words

fall asleep 眠りに落ちる noise 音、雑音 bathrobe バスローブ
thief 泥棒 run away 逃げる

1. Mika went to bed at 12:00 midnight*.
2. ______________________________.
3. ______________________________.
4. ______________________________.
5. ______________________________.
6. ______________________________.
7. ______________________________.
8. ______________________________.
9. ______________________________.
10. ______________________________.
11. ______________________________.
12. ______________________________.

*midnight 夜中

Grammar 2

71

Present Perfect

現在完了

Have you ever **had** a really bad experience*?	Yes, I **have**. I was bullied* in high school.
Have you ever **gone** overseas*?	Yes, I **have**. I went to Canada last summer.
Have you ever **failed** a test*?	Yes, I **have**. I didn't study for a math test, so I failed it.
Have you ever **met** a famous person?	Yes, I **have**. I met a famous sumo wrestler*.

*experience 経験　bully いじめる　overseas 海外　fail a test テストに落ちる、失敗する
sumo wrestler 相撲取り

▶Practice 5 Grammar: Simple Past and Past Participles 過去形と過去分詞

Write the simple past and past participle forms of the following verbs. The first one has been done for you.

以下の動詞の過去形と過去分詞形を書いてください。

Verb	Simple Past	Past Participle	Verb	Simple Past	Past Participle
1. buy	*bought*	*bought*	8. lose	______	______
2. eat	______	______	9. meet	______	______
3. feel	______	______	10. run	______	______
4. get	______	______	11. see	______	______
5. go	______	______	12. sleep	______	______
6. grow	______	______	13. stay	______	______
7. have	______	______	14. win	______	______

▶Practice 6 Writing: Have You Ever …? ライティング：～したことがありますか？

Write answers to the following questions. If you answer "yes", add an extra sentence as in the example.

以下の質問に答えましょう。もし答えが Yes なら、例を参考にして追加の文も作りましょう。

Example: A: Have you ever eaten a peanut butter sandwich?
B: Yes, I have. It was delicious. / I love peanut butter.
A: Have you ever seen a ghost?
B: No, I haven't.

1. Have you ever bought expensive clothes?

____

2. Have you ever gotten lost*?

____

3. Have you ever gone to a concert?

____

4. Have you ever slept in class?

____

5. Have you ever stayed up* all night?

____

*get lost まいごになる　stay up all night 一晩中起きている

▶Practice 7 Find Someone Who ... こんな人を探そう

First, complete the questions on the left of the chart below. Then find someone who answers "yes" to the first question and write their name on the right. After that, ask your second question and write notes about their answer. Talk to as many people as you can.

表の左側の質問文を完成させ、その質問に Yes（否定の質問で聞かれたら答えは No）と答えられる人を見つけたら、右側の欄に記入してください。できるだけ多くの人に質問しましょう。

Example: Question: Have you ever slept in class?
Answer: Yes, I have. (Write down the person's name.)
Question: Which class did you sleep in?
Answer: It was a high school math class. (Write "High school math class.")

Questions	Name / Note
1. Have ____________? (go overseas) Where ____________?	
2. Have ____________? (meet someone famous) Who ____________?	
3. Have ____________? (sleep in class) Which class ____________?	
4. Have ____________? (lose something important) What ____________?	
5. Have ____________? (win something) What ____________?	
6. Have ____________? (have a surprise birthday party) How old ____________?	
(Your idea) 7. Have ____________? ____________?	
(Your idea) 8. Have ____________? ____________?	

▶Practice 8 Reading: Memories リーディング：思い出

72

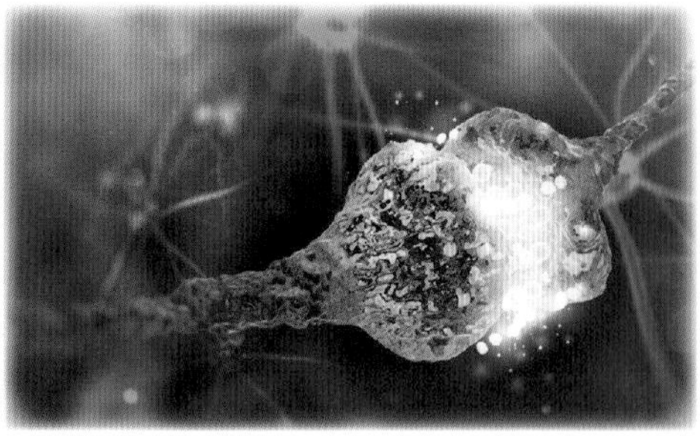

Memories are important to all of us: they affect* the way we think*, feel, and act*. Some people say that they cannot remember things easily, but we all can remember things we are interested in*. Some people cannot remember facts* in their school textbook, but they can remember details* about the players on their favorite baseball team. You probably* have something you are interested in and can remember details about it, whether* it is a television program, a song, or a hobby.

Your brain* is like a muscle*. If it isn't used, it becomes weaker* quickly*. Some people believe that older people have poorer* memories than younger people. However, research* shows just the opposite*. Younger people are usually more forgetful*. When young people forget something, like where they put their keys, they don't worry about it. When older people forget, they often worry they are losing* their memory because of age. If older people are active* and use their minds, they do not become senile* quickly.

* affect 影響する　the way we think 私達の考え方　act 行動する　interested in ～ ～に興味を持つ　fact 事実　detail 詳細　probably たぶん　whether ～ ～かどうか　brain 脳　muscle 筋肉　weaker より弱い　quickly 速く　poorer 乏しい、悪い　research 研究　opposite 反対の　forgetful 忘れっぽい　lose なくす　active 活動的　senile ぼけた

True or False 内容把握

Read the following sentences. Write T if the sentence is true and F if the sentence is false.

以下の文章が本文の内容と合っていれば "T"、合っていなければ "F" を空欄に入れましょう。

_____ 1. Most people have a bad memory.

_____ 2. People's interests affect how well they remember things.

_____ 3. If you use your memory a lot, it becomes weaker.

_____ 4. Younger people often have worse memories than older people.

_____ 5. It is good for older people to stay mentally active.

▶Practice 9 Group Work: Memory Challenge グループワーク：記憶力チャレンジ

Work with a partner. Look at the picture story in **Appendix 8** for two minutes. Try to remember the story and write the sentences in the correct order. Put the verbs in the past tense. The sixth sentence has already been done for you.

パートナーと Appendix 8 の絵を 2 分間見て、ストーリーの内容を覚えて下さい。そのあと、ストーリーの内容を表す英文に正しい順番をつけましょう。動詞はすべて過去形にして下さい。

Key Words

aliens 宇宙人	wave 手をふる	strange 不思議な
suddenly 突然	toward ～に向かって	ground 地面

(　　) He ________________ (run) outside to look, and one UFO ________________ (fly) over him.

(6) Inside the UFO, he ________________ (watch) two green aliens come towards him.

(　　) Zac ________________ (wake) up at night. There ________________ (is) a strange light in his room.

(　　) He ________________ (see) three UFOs in the sky.

(　　) He ________________ (wave) goodbye, and the UFO ________________ (fly) away.

(　　) They ________________ (take) him to another world. He ________________ (see) many new and strange things there.

(　　) Suddenly, he ________________ (fly) in the sky toward the UFO.

(　　) The aliens ________________ (bring) him back to Earth. He ________________ (return) to the ground near his house.

(　　) He ________________ (go) to the window and ________________ (look) outside.

(　　) The aliens ________________ (come) close and ________________ (speak) to him.

▶Practice 10 Sharing Memories 思い出をシェアする

Work in groups. Share one memory for each of the memory types below:

グループワーク：枠内のテーマでそれぞれの思い出をみんなでシェアしてみましょう。

A SCARY MEMORY 怖い思い出
A Sad Memory 悲しい想い出
A HAPPY MEMORY 幸せな思い出
An Early Memory 幼い時の思い出

▶Practice 11 Listening リスニング 73

Listen to the following presentation and write in the missing words below.

以下のプレゼンテーションを聞いて空欄を埋めましょう。

Hello everybody. Today, I'd like to ________________ my homestay experience. It happened* when ________________. I ________________ in Australia ________________. It was my first time ________________ and I was ________________. At first, I felt very homesick, so ________________ ________________ and ________________.

But my homestay family ________________, and gentle*. I went on family trips, and ________________ with my host sister. I ________________ confident*. Of course, I still* ________________, but I tried my best* and I started ________________. Because of that, ________________ ________. In the end*, I had such a good time* that ________________ to Japan!

I'll never ________________. After I graduate, I want to go back to Australia ________________ again.

Thank you very much ________________.

* happen 起こる　gentle 優しい　confident 自信のある　still いまだに　try one's best ベストを尽くす
in the end 最終的には　such a good time とても良い時間

▶Practice 12 Presentation プレゼンテーション

Prepare a presentation about an important event or person in your life that had an impact on you. You can use some of the language in **Practice 11**.

自分に最も影響を与えた出来事や人についてプレゼンテーションをしてみましょう。

Practice 11 を参考にしてください。

Unit 11

How Healthy Are You?

あなたの健康状態は？

Speaking

Practice the following dialogues with a partner.

以下の会話をパートナーと練習しましょう。

Dialogue 1 74

Mia: Hi, Steven. Are you alright*? You don't look so good.
Steven: I have a cold.
Mia: Oh, that's too bad. Do you have a fever?
Steven: No, but I have a sore throat* and a stuffy nose*.
Mia: Well, take care*.

Dialogue 2 75

Doctor: Have you ever had a serious illness* or injury*?
Mark: I was in a car accident* when I was in high school. I broke my leg.
Doctor: Oh, I see that in your medical history*. And what's your problem today?
Mark: I have a stomach ache*. It really hurts*.
Doctor: We'll give you some tests. Meanwhile*, drink this medicine and you'll feel better.
Mark: OK. Yuck*! This tastes* bad.

Dialogue 3 76

Janine: How did you hurt your head, Dana?
Dana: I fell down* some stairs*. It really hurt.
Janine: Did you see a doctor?
Dana: Yes. It was bleeding*, so he cleaned it and put on some Band-Aids.
Janine: Do you feel better now?
Dana: A little. I still* have a headache.

* alright 大丈夫　sore throat のどの痛み　stuffy nose 鼻づまり　take care お大事に
serious illness 深刻な病気　injury ケガ　car accident 交通事故　medical history 病歴
stomach ache 腹痛　hurt 痛む　meanwhile その間　yuck ゲー！　taste 味がする
fall down ころぶ　stairs 階段　bleed 出血する　still いまだに

Key Words: Symptoms 症状

Sickness 病気

fever 熱 influenza (the flu) インフルエンザ vomit (vomiting) 吐く
sweat (sweaty) 汗 (汗だくの)

Colds 風邪

sneeze (sneezing) くしゃみ (くしゃみをする) sore throat のどの痛み
cough (coughing) 咳 (咳をする) headache 頭痛

Other その他

backache 腰痛 stomach ache 腹痛 nosebleed 鼻血 rash 湿疹
toothache 歯痛 itch (itchy) かゆみ (かゆい)

►Practice 1 Symptoms 症状を説明する

Put the correct word from the box in the sentences below.

枠内から最も適切な表現を選んで、空欄に入れましょう。

toothache itchy fever dizzy* stomach ache
headache cough cold

* dizzy めまいがする

1. I have a ____________________.

2. My son has a ________________.

3. I have a bad ________________.

4. I have a ____________________.

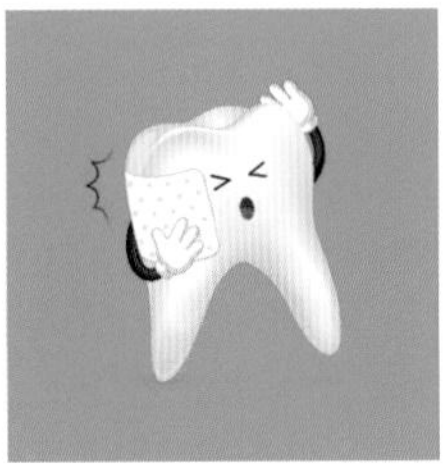

5. I have a ____________________.

6. I'm ____________________.

7. I have a ________________.

8. I'm ________________.

▶Practice 2 Listening: Symptoms リスニング：症状を聞く 78

Listen to the hints and circle the letter of the medical condition that is being described.

英文を聞いて説明にあう症状を選び、記号を○で囲みましょう。

1.	a) A stomach ache	b) A high fever	c) A cough	d) A headache
2.	a) A cough	b) Vomiting	c) A sneeze	d) A sore throat
3.	a) A headache	b) A backache*	c) A sore throat	d) A stomach ache
4.	a) A toothache	b) A backache	c) A stomach ache	d) A headache
5.	a) A nosebleed	b) A fever	c) A sore throat	d) A stomach ache
6.	a) Influenza	b) A rash	c) An itch	d) A toothache
7.	a) Sneeze	b) Sweat	c) Itch	d) Cough

* dentist 歯医者　　backache 腰痛

▶Practice 3 Verbs 動詞

Put the correct verb from the box in the sentences below. Use the present tense.

正しい動詞を枠内から選んで、現在形を入れてください。

have (use three times)　　be (use three times)　　hurt

1. I ________________ sick. I think I ________________ the flu.
2. I have an allergy*. My arm ________________ itchy.
3. Satsuki ____________ a cough.
4. I ________________ a toothache. My tooth* ________________.
5. I ________________ dizzy.

* allergy アレルギー　　tooth 歯

Key Words: Parts of the Body

79

Look at the words for the parts of the body below and try to remember them.

以下の体の部分の名前を覚えましょう。

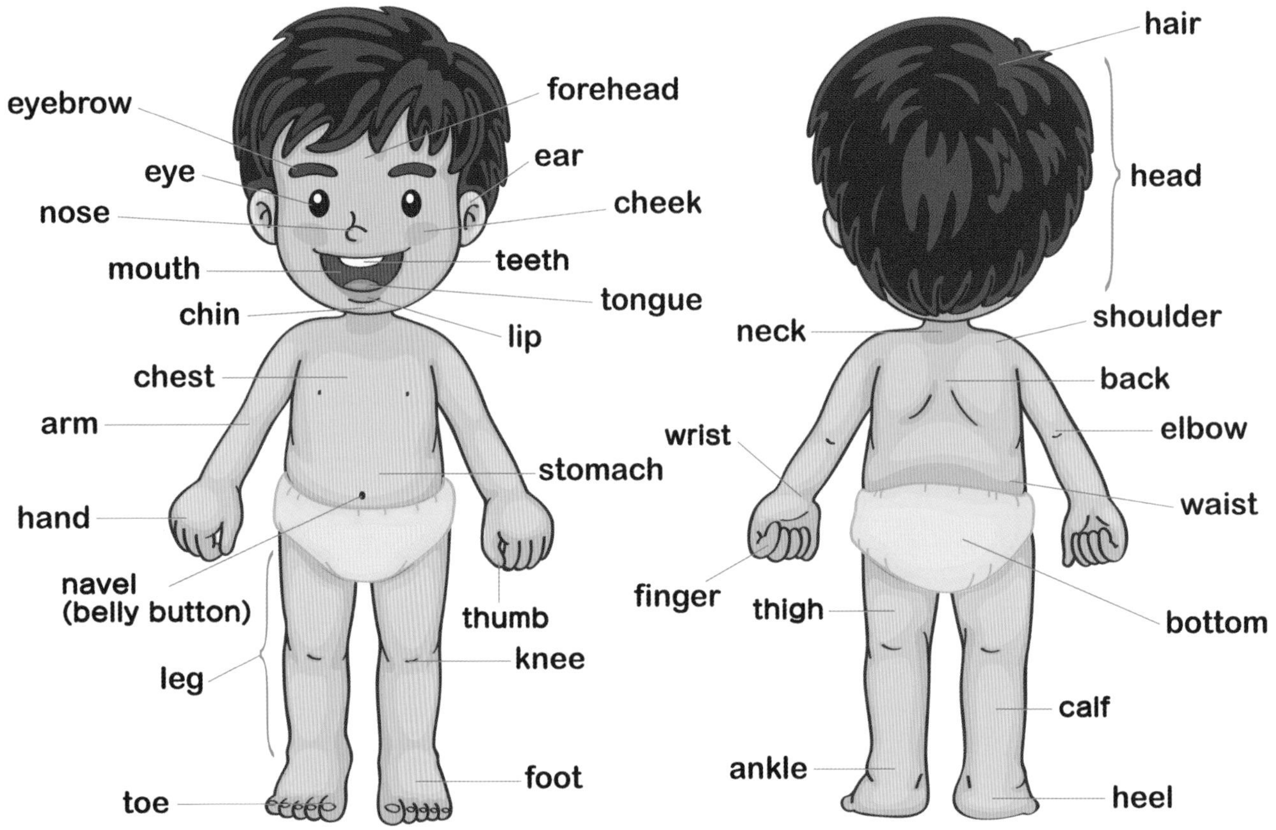

►Practice 4 Pair Work: Memory Check ペアワーク：どのくらい覚えてる？

Work in pairs. How many words for parts of the body can you remember? Turn to **Appendix 9** and label the parts of the body.

どのくらい体の部分の名前を覚えたか、パートナーといっしょに Appendix 9 を開いて空欄を埋めてみましょう。

►Practice 5 Pair Work: Questions About the Body ペアワーク：体についての質問

Use words from Parts of the Body to answer the following questions.

“Parts of the Body” を参考にして、以下の質問に答えましょう。

Example:	Question:	We taste with this part of the body.
	Answer:	Tongue.

1. What do boys have on top of* their head that some men don’t have? ____________________.
2. What part of the body opens and closes when you eat? ____________________.
3. What is in the middle of your leg, between your thigh and your calf? ____________________.

4. What is the part of the body between your head and your shoulders? ________________.
5. What part of the body do we use to smell*? ________________.
6. Each of your hands has five of these. ________________.
7. Each of your feet has five of these. ________________.
8. We see with these. ________________.
9. Your heart is inside your ... ________________.
10. What is the name of your shortest and fattest* finger? ________________.

* on top of ～ ～の上に　smell 臭いをかぐ　fattest 一番太った

▶Practice 6 Parts of the Body Bingo 体の部分の名前でビンゴ

Select 12 body words from the choices below and write them in the Bingo Card. Then listen to your teacher describe different body parts. Cross off the words corresponding to the hints. When you have crossed off four words in a row on your card, shout "Bingo!"

枠内から 12 の体の部分名を選んで、ビンゴカードに書きましょう。先生がその体の部分の説明をするので、それに合う部分名を線で消し、消した単語が縦か横に 4 つ並んだら "Bingo!" と叫びましょう。

leg　lip　thumb　toe　ear　eye　knee　hand　neck　mouth
chest　back　nose　head　shoulder　ankle　wrist　foot

Bingo Card

▶Practice 7 Word Practice 文法問題

Put the correct word from the box in the sentences below. Change the verbs to the correct tense.

それぞれの枠内から最も適切な単語を選んで、空欄を埋めましょう。動詞は最も適切な形に変えてください。

Verbs 動詞

cut 切る　bleed 出血する　break 折る　sprain 捻挫する　burn ヤケドする　hurt 痛める

Nouns 名詞

bruise 青アザ

Adjectives 形容詞

dizzy めまいがする

1. I have a ______________ on my arm.

2. Oh, no! You ______________ your leg.

3. I ______________ myself when I touched a hot pan.

4. I fell down and hit my head. I feel ______________.

5. I ______________ my ankle* when running. It ______________ when I walk.

6. I ______________ my hand with a knife and it's ______________.

* ankle 足首

▶Practice 8 Complete the Story: Kara's Accident ストーリーを完成させる：Kara の事故

Complete the story about Kara's accident. Use the words in the box. Change the verbs to the past tense.

Kara の事故についてストーリーを完成させてください。枠内の表現を使って、動詞は適切な形に変えましょう。

Verbs

go tell fall down stay

Other Words

leg hospital stairs* ambulance* broken

* stairs 階段 ambulance 救急車

Kara  ______________ ______________ some ______________.

She ______________ to the  ______________ by  ______________.

The doctor  ______________ her that she had a 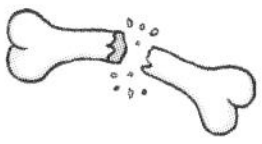 ______________

 ______________. She ______________ in the hospital for two weeks.

Grammar

80

Modal Verbs 助動詞

Modals of Advice ～したほうがよい

You ***should*** avoid* fatty food*.

You ***had better*** avoid fatty food.

You ***ought to**** avoid fatty food.

You ***should not*** eat fatty food.

You ***had better not*** eat fatty food.

Should I avoid fatty food?

Modals of Necessity ～しなければならない

You ***must*** eat a balanced diet*.

You ***have got to*** eat a balanced diet.

You ***have to*** eat a balanced diet.

You ***mustn't*** eat so much sugar.

Do I ***have to*** avoid sugar?

* "**Ought to**" is rarely used in the negative form.

** "**Ought**" and "**had better**" are rarely used in questions.

* avoid 避ける　fatty foods 脂っこい食べ物　balanced diet バランスの取れた食生活
ought to ～ / had better ～ ～しなければならない

►Practice 9 Listening リスニング

81

Listen to the dialogue and write in the missing words.

会話を聞いて空欄を埋めましょう。

Miwa: ______________________ this health questionnaire* on the internet?

Roger: No, I didn't. Go ahead and ______________________ of the questions.

Miwa: OK. ____________________________________ or exercise*?

Roger: Hardly ever. I ______________________ and sports.

Miwa: That's not good. ______________________ exercise.

Roger: No way! __________________________.

Miwa: Do you __________________________?

Roger: Not really. I love _______________________________.

Miwa: That's really bad. You ______________________ healthier food.

Roger: Yeah, I know. But ______________________.

Miwa: You _______________________________ of vegetables every day.

Roger: OK, stop! I've heard enough. I'm hungry. ______________________!

* health questionnaire 問診表　exercise 運動（する）

▶Practice 10 Giving Advice アドバイスをする

What advice would you give to the following people?

以下のような問題をかかえた人たちにどんなアドバイスをしますか

1. I need to lose weight*.

   Your advice: ______________________________.

2. I want to run in the Tokyo Marathon.

   Your advice: ______________________________.

3. I have diabetes*. Is it OK to eat ice cream and other desserts?

   Your advice: ______________________________.

4. I eat mostly fast food.

   Your advice: ______________________________.

5. I need to improve* my English.

   Your advice: ______________________________.

6. I want to get rich.

   Your advice: ______________________________.

* lose weight 体重を減らす　diabetes 糖尿病　improve 改善する

▶Practice 11 How Healthy Are You? どのくらい健康ですか？

Read the following questions and choose the answer that is truest for you. Then ask the questions to your partner.

以下の質問に答えてみましょう。そのあとパートナーにも聞いてみましょう。

1. Which would you usually choose for breakfast?

A.

B.

C.

D.

2. Which would you usually choose for lunch?

A.

B.

C.

3. Which would you usually choose for dinner?

A.

B.

C.

4. Which would you choose for snacks or desert?

A.

B.

C.

D.

E.

F.

5. How much water and healthy drinks do you have each day?

A. Six glasses or more

B. Around* four glasses

C. Three glasses or less*

6. How often do you exercise each week?

A. Three times a week or more
B. Once or twice a week
C. Hardly ever
D. Never

7. How much sleep do you get each night on average?

A. Under six hours
B. Six to seven hours
C. Around eight hours
D. Over eight hours

* around だいたい　less ～以下

8. How often do you walk or bicycle each day?

A. Over* one hour
B. 30 minutes to one hour
C. Less than* 30 minutes

9. How often do you feel stressed?

A. Very often
B. Often
C. Sometimes
D. Rarely

* over～ ～以上　less than～ ～以下

▶Practice 12 Pair Work: At the Doctors ペアワーク：お医者さんとの会話

Write one dialogue between a doctor and a patient with your partner. After you finish, prepare to act your dialogue in front of the class. You may talk about the following things:

医者と患者の会話をパートナーと考えてみてください。その会話をクラスメイトの前で発表してみましょう。以下のリストを参考にしてください。

* A medical problem (accident or sickness)	* Diet	* Sleep
* Medical history (Have you ever ...)	* Exercise	* Stress

Unit 12

You Can Fly!

君も飛べるよ

Speaking

Practice the following dialogues with a partner. After you have practiced the model conversation a few times, substitute the underlined information with the words in the boxes.

以下の会話をパートナーと練習してください。数回練習したら，下線の部分を枠内の表現に言いかえて再度練習しましょう。

Dialogue 1 82

Tina: What are you studying, Emi?

Emi: I'm studying for an English test. I don't like English and I hate tests.

Tina: Do you want me to help you?(1)

Emi: No. It's a waste of time*.

Tina: Why do you say that?

Emi: Because I'm not good(2) at* English. I don't need to learn English anyway.

Tina: But it might be useful in the future, either at work or if you travel overseas*.

Emi: Umm... I don't think so. I don't even* know what I want to do in the future.

Tina: Emi, you should try to be more positive*(3).

*waste of time 時間の無駄　be good at ～ ～が得意　travel overseas 海外に旅行する　even ～ ～さえ　positive 前向きな

1. Can I help you? Shall I help you?	2. useless at* terrible at*	3. think more positively* be less* negative*

*useless at ～ ～には役に立たない　terrible at ～はとても苦手　positively 前向きに　less ～より～ない　negative 悲観的な

Dialogue 2 83

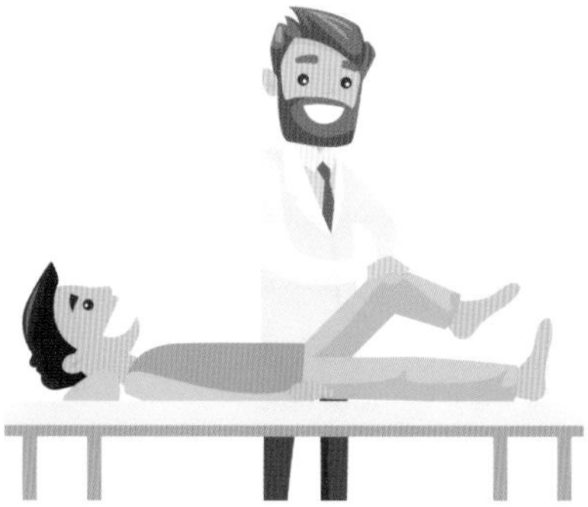

Blake: What's your major, Ken?

Ken: Health and physical education.* I want to be a physical therapist* in the future.

Blake: Oh, yeah?

Ken: Yeah, I'm really interested in* helping people with physical problems.(1)

Blake: How come?*

Ken: Well, I had a car accident* when I was a kid* and physical therapy really helped me. I'd like to help other people in the same way.*

Blake: That's great!(2) Is studying physical therapy difficult?

Ken: Yeah, at times,* but I enjoy learning about the body and health. I want to(3) be a good physical therapist in the future.

* health and physical education 保健医療学　physical therapist 理学療法士
interested in～ ～に興味がある　how come? なぜ？　accident 事故　kid 子ども
in the same way 同じように　at times ときに

1. I'm really excited about I can't wait to start	2. wonderful terrific*	3. I'm determined to* I hope I can

* terrific すばらしい　be determined to～ ～すると固く決意している

▶Practice 1 Let's Discuss Together みんなで考えてみよう

Look at the image of the glass. Some people might* say "the glass is half full.*" Other people might say "the glass is half empty.*" People who see the glass half full are called "optimists,*" and those who see it half empty are called "pessimists*".

* might かもしれない　half full 半分入っている
half empty 半分カラの　optimist 楽観主義者
pessimist 悲観主義者

Now look back at the two dialogues in **Speaking**. Discuss the following questions.
Dialogue 1 と Dialogue 2 を見て、以下の質問に答えましょう。

1. Who do you think is a pessimist, Emi or Ken? Why?
2. Who do you think is an optimist? Why?
3. Which person might be more successful* in the future, Emi or Ken? Why?
4. When you look at the glass of water, what do you see? Is the glass half empty or half full?
5. Are you an optimist or a pessimist?
6. Do you think it is possible* to change from a pessimist to an optimist?

* successful 成功した possible 可能な

▶Practice 2 Mindset Quiz マインドセットクイズ

Read the statements and then check the box that is most correct for you.
表の左側の文を読み、程度を示す欄の中で自分に最も合っているものをチェックしてください。

	Strongly Agree*	Agree*	Disagree*	Strongly Disagree*
1. I like to study because I want to learn new things.	□	□	□	□
2. Smart* people do not need to try hard.	□	□	□	□
3. I like to challenge* new things.	□	□	□	□
4. I feel good when my friends are successful.	□	□	□	□
5. I give up* easily* when I'm not successful.	□	□	□	□
6. I get really hurt* when I look stupid*.	□	□	□	□
7. I learn a lot from my mistakes.	□	□	□	□
8. You can change your personality*.	□	□	□	□

* strongly agree 非常にそう思う agree そう思う disagree そう思わない
strongly disagree 全くそう思わない smart 頭の良い、賢い challenge 挑戦する
give up あきらめる easily 簡単に hurt 傷つく look stupid 間抜けに見える personality 性格

Grammar

84

Gerunds and Infinitives

動名詞と不定詞

Gerunds 動名詞	**Infinitives** 不定詞
I like ***listening*** to music.	I like ***to listen*** to music.
I love ***traveling***.	I love ***to travel***.
She began ***studying*** English.	She began ***to study*** English.
He finished* ***cleaning*** his room.	I want* ***to play*** tennis.

Gerunds as Subjects

Learning a new language is difficult.

Challenging new things is good for you.

* "finish" は動名詞しかとらない　"want" は不定詞しかとらない

▶Practice 3 Grammar (1)

Look at the sentences and write the gerund, the infinitive, or both according to the verb given.

カッコ内の動詞を不定詞か動名詞のどちらかに変えて入れましょう。

Example: He likes *going / to go* (go) shopping on weekends.

1. I like ____________________ (play) tennis.
2. I finished ____________________ (write) the report.
3. The student was sick and wanted ____________________ (go) home.
4. She asked me ____________________ (help) her.
5. He began ____________________ (play) the piano.
6. They want ____________________ (talk) about school, but I want ____________________ (watch) TV.
7. I started ____________________ (study) after dinner and then stopped ____________________ (study) at 11 p.m.

▶Practice 4 Grammar (2) 文法の練習問題

Write sentences that are true for you.

自分について文章を作りましょう。

Gerunds

1. I love ______________________.
2. I hate ______________________.
3. I began ______________________.
4. ________________ is difficult for me.
5. ________________ is a lot of fun.

Infinitives

1. I love ______________________.
2. I hate ______________________.
3. After getting home*, I want ______________________.
4. On weekends, I don't want ______________________.

※ get home 家に着く

▶Practice 5 Reading: Mindset リーディング：マインドセット 85

Do you sometimes have thoughts* like "I can't speak English," "I'm not good at math," or "I'm not good at sports"? These thoughts can hurt you. They can stop you from making progress* in life. This kind of negative thinking is called "a fixed mindset*." People who believe that they can learn new skills by trying their best* have "a growth mindset*."

Carol Dweck, a psychologist* at Stanford University, is famous for* writing about "fixed mindset" and "growth mindset." People with a fixed mindset think they cannot change their intelligence or learn new skills. People with a growth mindset know they can learn new skills if they try hard. They can even become more intelligent*. Our minds are very powerful. Our thoughts can help us grow or they can stop us from challenging new things.

If you have a fixed mindset, you are afraid of failure*. You want to look good all the time so that no one criticizes* you. Therefore, you avoid* new challenges or do not try hard. As a result*, you do not learn new skills. But if you have a growth mindset, you know failure is a part of learning new things. You do not give up easily. You learn from mistakes and criticism*.

Can a person with a fixed mindset change? Yes! Just take small steps. Challenge yourself to keep going when you fail* or make mistakes. When you make progress*, your confidence* will increase*. Then you will not be afraid of* new challenges and can fly!

* thoughts 考え　make progress 進歩する　fixed mindset 硬直マインドセット
try one's best ベストを尽くす　growth mindset しなやかマインドセット　psychologist 心理学者
famous for ～ ～で有名　intelligent 知的な　failure 失敗　criticize 批判する　avoid 避ける
as a result 結果として　criticism 批判　fail 失敗する　progresss 進歩する
confidence 自信　increase 増す　be afraid of ～ ～を恐れる

True or False 内容把握

Write "T" for true or "F" for false for each of the sentences below.

以下の文章が本文の内容と合っていれば "T"、合っていなければ "F" を空欄に入れましょう。

_____ 1. Having a fixed mindset helps us get new skills.

_____ 2. Carol Dweck believes intelligence cannot change.

_____ 3. People with a growth mindset like new challenges.

_____ 4. People with a fixed mindset are afraid of failure.

_____ 5. If you have a fixed mindset, you can change it to a growth mindset.

_____ 6. If you want to change, it's best to start taking big steps.

_____ 7. If you learn one skill, it can help you to learn other skills.

Mindset Chart マインドセットチャート

How you feel about ... こんなことに直面したらどう感じますか?	Growth Mindset しなやかマインドセット	Fixed Mindset 硬直マインドセット
Challenges 挑戦	You want to keep learning 学び続けたい You accept challenges 挑戦をいとわない	You want to look smart 自分は有能だと思われたい You avoid challenges 挑戦することを避ける
Difficulties and mistakes 障害や失敗	Keep trying トライし続ける You think about how to do better よりうまくなるために考える	You give up easily すぐあきらめる You blame* others 人のせいにする
Criticism 批評	You learn from critism and mistakes 失敗やミスから学ぶ	You get hurt and become angry すぐに傷つき怒りを覚える
Success of people around you 周りの人の成功	You are happy to learn from others' success 他の人の成功から学びたいと思う	You feel bad and get jealous 他の人の成功を脅威と感じ嫉妬する

* blame～ ～のせいにする

▶Practice 6 Fixed or Growth Mindset?

Look at the various thoughts below, and then put the letters in the chart under "Fixed Mindset" or "Growth Mindset." The first one has been done for you.

枠内には様々な "感情" のリストがあります。Fixed Mindset か Growth Mindset に分けてみましょう。

* impossible 不可能　　naturally 生まれつき、もともと　　stupid バカな

Fixed Mindset			Growth Mindset		
1. A	3. ______	5. ______	1. ______	3. ______	5. ______
2. ______	4. ______		2. ______	4. ______	

▶Practice 7 Running Dictation: The Story of Mina ケーススタディ：Mina の場合

You are now going to do a running dictation. Listen carefully to your teacher's instructions and have fun in this contest. Good luck!

ディクテーションゲームをしましょう。先生の説明をよく聞いてゲームを楽しみましょう。Good luck!

▶Practice 8 Group Discussion: Hitting a Wall グループ・ディスカッション：壁にぶち当たったら

A

B

1. Which man has a fixed mindset and which has a growth mindset? Why?
   Fixed Mindset の人、Growth Mindset の人はどちらでしょう？
   それはなぜですか？
2. Do you have a fixed mindset about some things in your life? What are they?
   生活の中で自分が fixed mindset になっているときはありますか？
   それはなぜですか？
3. Can you think of a "wall" in your life that you faced? Did you break through it successfully?
   今まで壁にぶち当たったことはありますか？それは打破できましたか？

▶Practice 9 Writing: Developing English Skills ライティング：英語のスキルをみがく

Imagine you will move to England next year. What can you do to improve your English communication skills before your move? Write down several ideas below, using "I can ...."

来年イギリスに引っ越すことになりました。その前に英語のコミュニケーションスキルを磨くためにどんなことをすればよいですか？以下にアイデアを書きましょう。I can ～を使いましょう。

Example: I can watch movies in English.

1. ______________________________.
2. ______________________________.
3. ______________________________.
4. ______________________________.
5. ______________________________.
6. ______________________________.

What do you think about your English? Can you become good at English? Why or why not?

自分の英語力をどう思いますか？英語がうまくなると思いますか？なぜそう思うのですか？

▶Practice 10 Listening リスニング 86

Listen to the story and fill in the missing words.

英語のストーリーを聞いて空欄を埋めましょう。

Today I'll tell you about a ____________ who made many animation movies and cartoons*. His most famous character ____________. Do ____________? Of course, it's Walt Disney.

He ____________ in Chicago ____________. He loved ____________ and ____________ when he ____________. He started an animation company ____________, but it lost money and he had ____________.

He moved to Hollywood and ____________. He made a character called Oswald the Lucky Rabbit, which ____________. But a business partner stole* the character and took away ____________. Disney was shocked, but ____________.

In 1928, ____________ Mickey Mouse movie. It was very popular and ____________. He worked hard and ____________, such as "Snow White," "Cinderella," and "Bambi". ____________ Disneyland, a theme park* near Los Angeles.

Walt Disney died* in 1966 when ____________. However, ____________ remember him and still ____________.

* cartoons アニメ(番組)、マンガ　steal 盗む
theme park テーマパーク　die 死ぬ

▶Practice 11 Presentation: Road to Success 成功への道

You will give a presentation about a person who faced difficult times but was finally successful. This person could be a family member, a friend, or someone who is famous. Look at the story of Walt Disney in **Practice 10** as an example.

自分の周りの人たちで、困難な課題に直面したにもかかわらず成功した人たちについてプレゼンテーションをしてみましょう。Practice 10 と枠内の表現を参考にしてください。

▶Practice 1 Group Work: Who's Telling the Truth? 真実を語っているのは誰？

First, write about an interesting experience you had, for example, a place you visited, a famous person you saw, or an accident you had. Write one sentence.

自分のユニークな経験（訪れた場所、会ったことのある有名人、事故や記憶に残る出来事など）について書きましょう。

Interesting experience: ______________________________

Share your story with other students in your group. The group chooses the most interesting one. All members in your group will stand in front of the class and share the same story, but only one person is telling the truth. The class will ask questions to see who is telling the truth. Have fun!

自分のストーリーを同じグループ内の人とシェアして、最も興味深いストーリーを選んで下さい。そのグループの人たちはクラスメイトの前に立ち、同じストーリーをシェアします。でもグループ内の一人だけが本当のことを言っています。誰が真実を語っているか、当てましょう。

Example: Student A: "I ate horsemeat." Student B: "I ate horsemeat."
Student C: "I ate horsemeat." Student D: "I ate horsemeat."

Question: "Where did you eat horsemeat?"
Student A: "I ate it in Kyoto." (not true)
Student B: "I ate it in New York." (not true)
Student C: "I ate it in Hakone." (true)
Student D: "I ate it at my grandmother's house in Tokyo." (not true)

▶Practice 2 Listening 87

Listen to the conversation between Kelly and Andy and answer the questions below.

1. What was wrong with Andy? ______________________________
2. What were his symptoms*? ______________________________
3. How many days of school did he miss*? ______________________________
4. How much of the report has Andy written? ______________________________
5. Do you think Andy has a growth or a fixed mindset? ______________________________

* symptoms 症状　miss 欠席する

Review Units 10 - 12

▶Practice 3 Board Game ボードゲーム

To play the board game below, you will need to make groups. Follow the instructions.
以下のルールに従って、グループでボードゲームをしてみましょう。

1. Use small pieces of paper with your initials on them as markers.
小さな紙に自分のイニシャルを書き，自分の駒にします。
2. Toss a coin or play 'rock, paper, scissors' to decide who goes first.
コインを使って（またはジャンケンで）誰から始めるかを決めます。

START HERE

1. Where are you from? Tell us about it.

2. What kind of movies do you like?

3. What kind of music do you like?

4. What do you love doing?

5. What do you hate doing?

6. What's your least favorite food?

7. Say as many adjectives* to describe* somebody's personality as you can in 20 seconds.

8. Tell us about your family.

9. Compare* your elementary school* and your high school.

10. How are you feeling today?

11. What did you do on your last vacation?

12. What did you eat for breakfast this morning?

13. What's your happiest memory? Tell us about it.

3. Each player then takes turns by tossing a coin. If the coin lands face up, move two spaces. If the coin lands face down, move one space.
順番にコインを投げ、表が出たら２マス、裏か出たら１マス進みます。
4. When you land on a space, answer the question. Answer any follow-up questions.
出たマスの質問に答え，追加の質問にも答えます。

Useful expressions: 便利な表現：

I'll go first.　最初に行います。　　Is it my turn?　私の番ですか？　　It's your turn.　あなたの番です。

22. What are you not good at?

23. What can you do to become better at English?

24. Are you an optimist or a pessimist?

GOAL!

21. What are you good at?

20. Tell us about your best friend (try to speak for 30 seconds without stopping).

19. Do you think you are healthy? Why or why not?

18. What unhealthy* things do you eat and drink?

17. What healthy things do you eat and drink?

14. How much money did you spend yesterday?

15. Have you ever been to Disneyland? Tell us about it.

16. What's your favorite animation character? Why?

* adjective 形容詞　　describe 説明する
compare 比べる　　elementary school 小学校　　unhealthy 不健康な

Appendix 1

Karen's Working Day　カレンの仕事

Student B

Work with **Student A**. Ask and answer questions to find the missing information in Karen's schedule.

お互いに質問し合い，カレンの予定を埋めましょう。

Example: Question: What does Karen do at 6 a.m.? Answer: She wakes up (at 6 a.m.).
Question: When does Karen wake up? Answer: (She wakes up) At 6.a.m.

Time	Activity
6 a.m.	Karen wakes up.
	Karen eats breakfast.
7 a.m.	Karen leaves home.
7:30 a.m. – 8:40 a.m.	
8:50 a.m.	Karen arrives* at her office.
	Karen drinks a cup of tea.
9 a.m. – 9:30 a.m.	Karen has a meeting with her boss.
9:30 a.m. – 9:45 a.m.	
9:45 a.m. – 12 noon	Karen works at her desk.
	Karen eats lunch.
1 p.m. – 2 p.m.	Karen has a meeting with her co-workers.
2 p.m. – 5:30 p.m.	
5:30 p.m. – 5:55 p.m.	Karen plans tomorrow's schedule.
	Karen leaves* the office.
6 p.m. – 6:10 p.m.	Karen walks to the station.
6:10 p.m. – 7:20 p.m.	
7:25 p.m.	Karen buys* food at the supermarket.
	Karen arrives home and cooks dinner.
9 p.m.	Karen surfs the internet and watches TV.
10:30 p.m.	
11 p.m.	Karen goes to bed.

*arrive 着く　leave 出る、去る　buy 買う

Appendix 2

Find the Differences　違いを探そう

Student B

Student A: Look at the picture below. Tell your partner what is happening in your picture. Find 9 differences between your picture and your partner's.

Student A は p.21 の絵を見て、Student B は以下の絵を見て下さい。パートナーにお互い自分が見ている絵を説明し、違いを 9 つ見つけましょう。

Example:

Student A:　In my picture Mr. Kubo's reading a letter.

Student B:　Oh, really? In my picture Mr. Kubo's reading a book.

Picture B

Appendix 3

Nationality and Language 国籍と言語

Student B

Take turns and ask questions. Write down the answers in the blanks below, as shown in the example.

交代でお互いに質問をし、空欄に正しい国名、言語を入れましょう。

Example: Student A: Where's Yelena from?
Student B: She's from Russia.
Student A: How do you spell "Russia"?
Student B: "R-U-S-S-I-A." What's her nationality*?
Student A: She's Russian. What language does she speak?
Student B: She speaks Russian.

* nationality 国籍

Name	Country	Nationality	Language
1. Yelena (she)	*Russia*	*Russian*	*Russian*
2. Charlotte (she)	______	British	______
3. Min-jun (he)	______	______	Korean
4. Mai (she)	Vietnam	______	Vietnamese
5. Somchai (he)	______	Thai	Thai
6. Adam (he)	The United States	______	______
7. Yun (she)	______	Chinese	______
8. Miguel (he)	Brazil	______	Portuguese

Appendix 4

The Story of Kim　ペアワーク：Kim のストーリー

Student B

Work in pairs. Ask questions to get the information you need to fill in the spaces below.
カッコ内の単語を使って、パートナーに質問しながら空欄を埋めましょう。

Example:　A: What does he like to do in his free time?
B: He likes to play …

Kim is from Korea. He's a (1) ____________________ (what / do) but he works part-time, too. He studies computer engineering at the University of Seoul. Kim is (2) ____________________ (how old) and is a (3) ____________________ (what year in university / he). His favorite class is called Introduction to Software Design*. He wants to (4) ____________________ (what / do / future) in the future. Kim speaks Korean, of course, but he also speaks (5) ____________________ and ____________________ (what other languages / speak). He plans to study in Japan next year. He already has some Japanese friends that he met online. He's looking forward to meeting them in Japan. He likes to (6) ____________________ (what / like to do / free time) in his free time.

* Introduction to Software Design　ソフトウェアデザイン入門

Appendix 5

Crossword クロスワード

Student B

Give hints to help your partner guess the words that you can see in your half of the crossword. But do not say the actual words in your hints. Then listen to your partner and write in the words that he / she is describing.

ペアになって，Student A はこのページを参照し，Student B は Appendix 3 を参照します。クロスワードの埋まっている単語 のヒントを出し合い，お互いの空欄を埋めて完成させましょう。

Example: A: What's 9 down?
B: It's a house, a place that people live in with their families.
A: A home?
B: That's right! Now, what's 2 across?
A: It's the same as "personality".

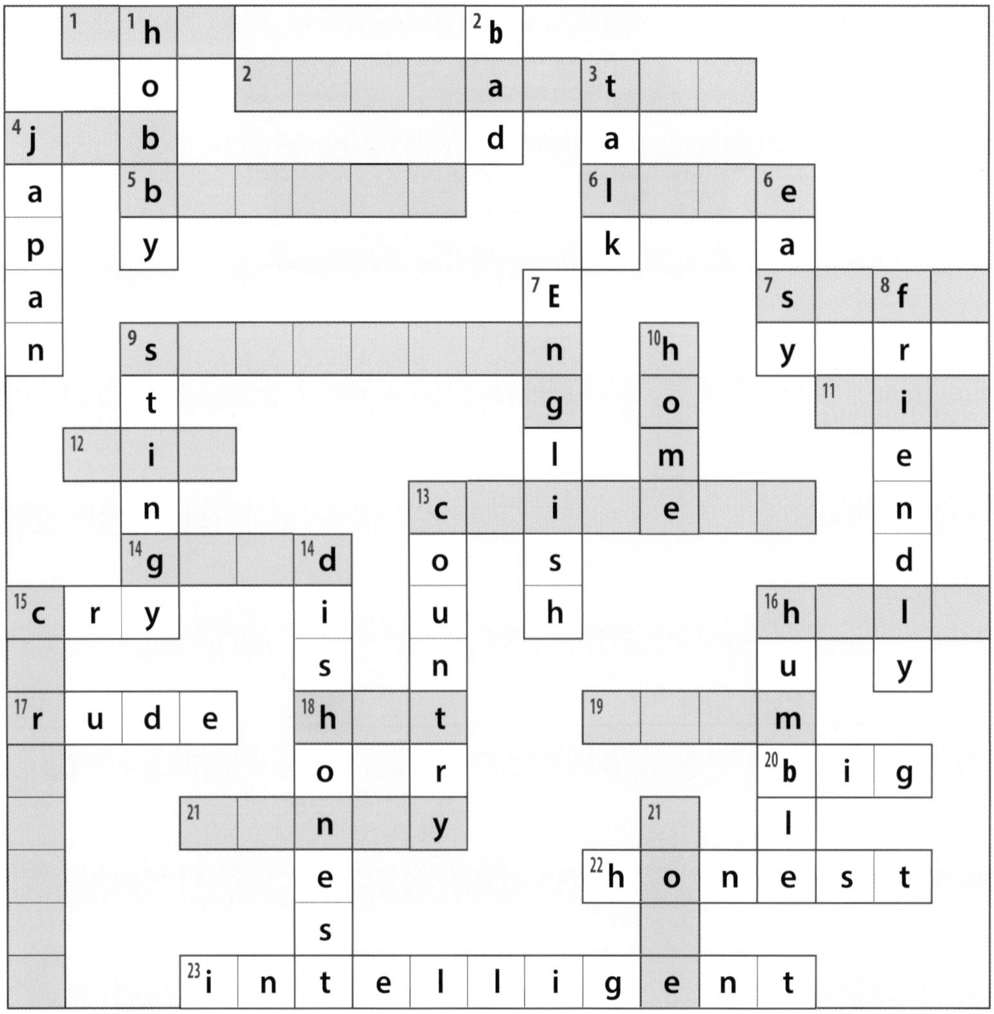

Appendix 6

Family Tree (Part 2) 家系図　パート2

Student B

There are 15 differences in the family tree. Ask questions to **Student A** to find the differences.

Student A は p.71 の絵を見てください。Student B は以下の絵を見てください。2人のみている Trevor の家系図には 15 か所異なる点があります。お互いに質問しながら違いを見つけましょう。

Examples: What's Steven's last name? What does Trevor do?
How old's Steven's wife? What's Steven's wife's name?

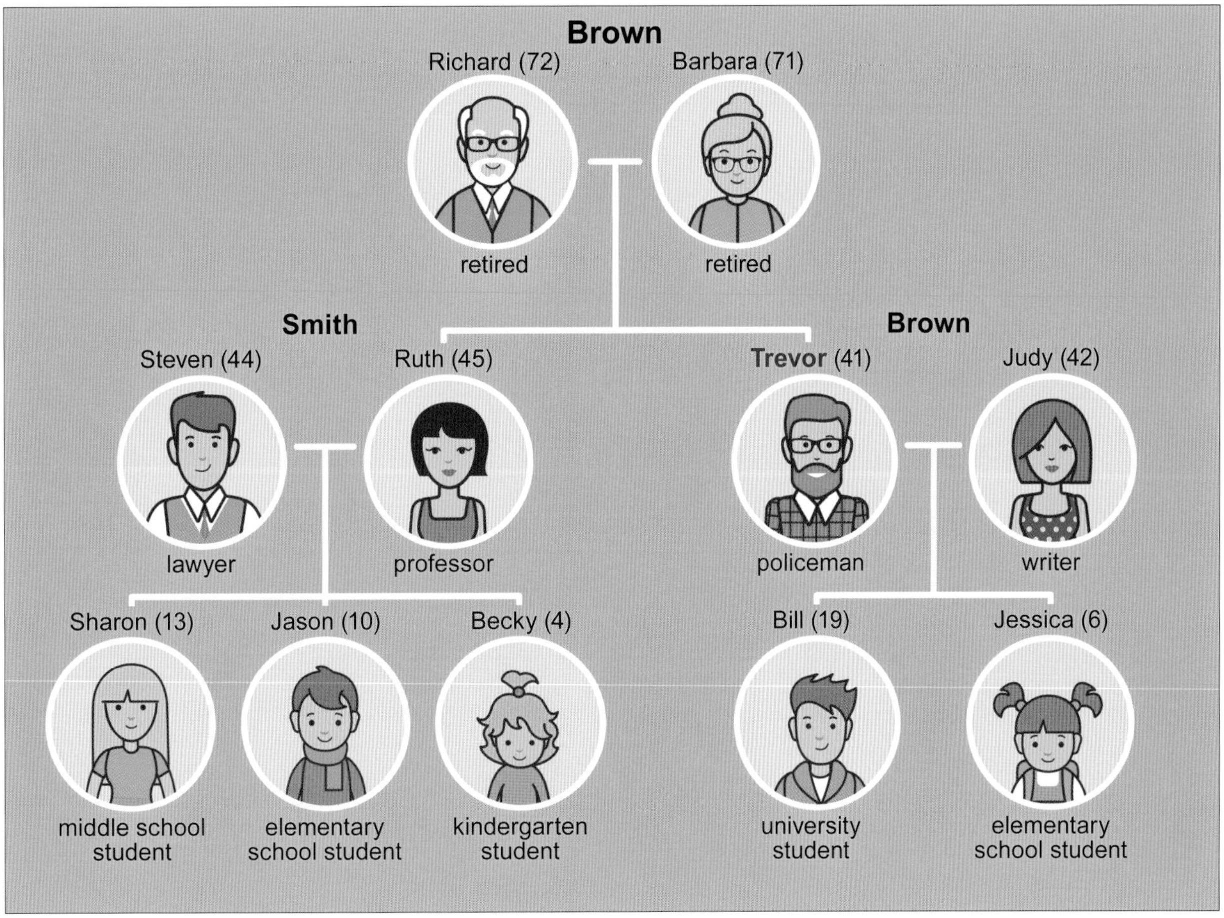

Appendix 7

Crossword クロスワード

Student B

Give hints to help your partner guess the words that you can see in your half of the crossword. But do not say the actual words in your hints. Then listen to your partner and write in the words that he / she is describing.

クロスワードの埋まっている単語 のヒントを出し合い，お互いの空欄を埋めて完成させましょう。

Example: B: What's "4 across"?
A: This is something you send online to friends and family.
B: Pictures? Email?
A: No, these are often just a few words. Text…
B: Message!
A: Yes, that's it!

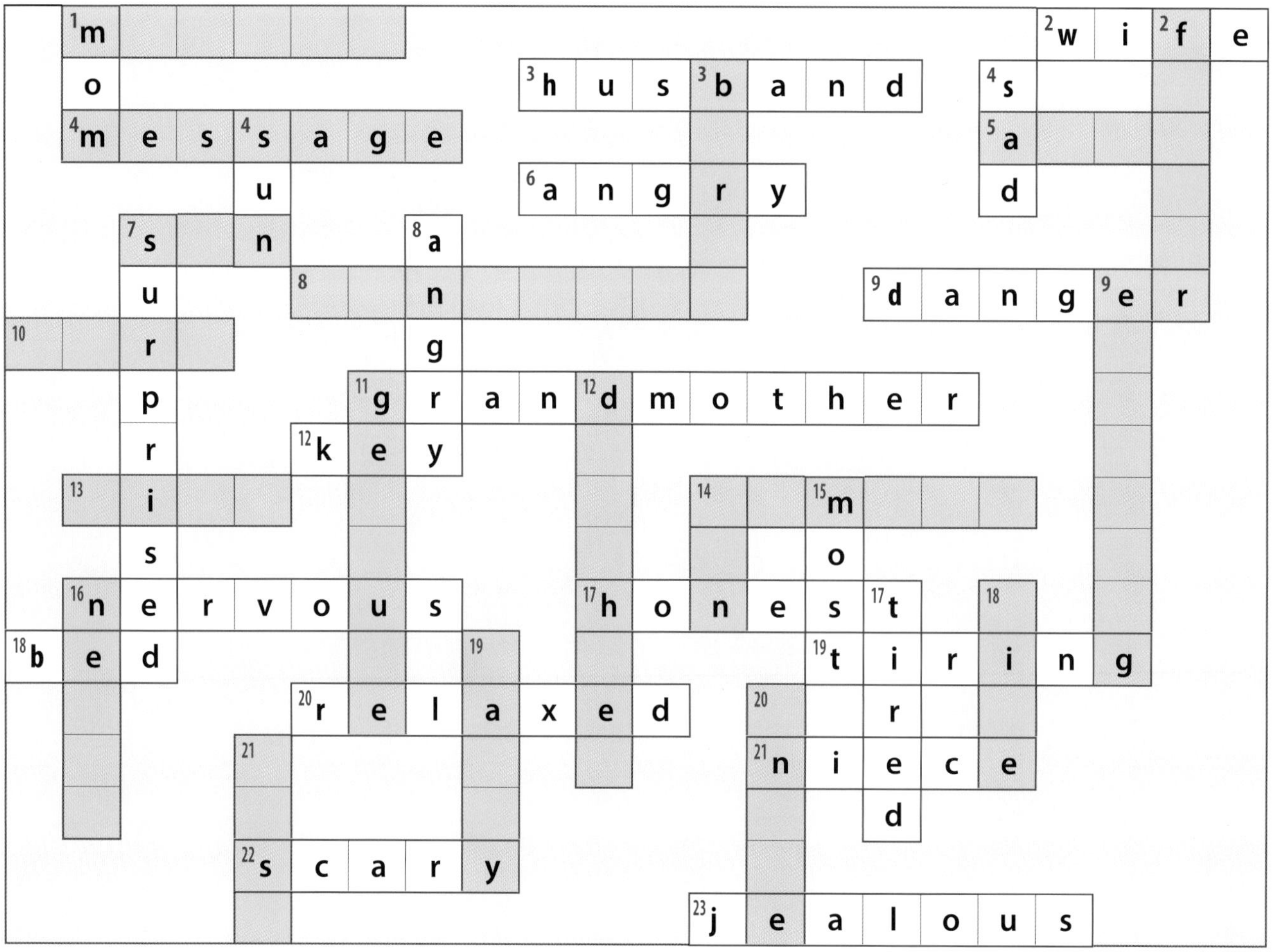

Appendix 8

Group Work: Memory Challenge　グループワーク：記憶力チャレンジ

1.

2.

3.

4.

5.

6.

7.

8.
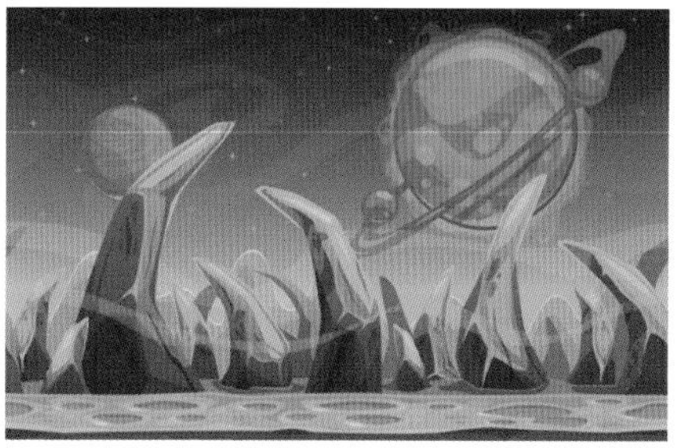

9.

10.

Appendix 9

Memory Check　どのくらい覚えてる？

Parts of the Body

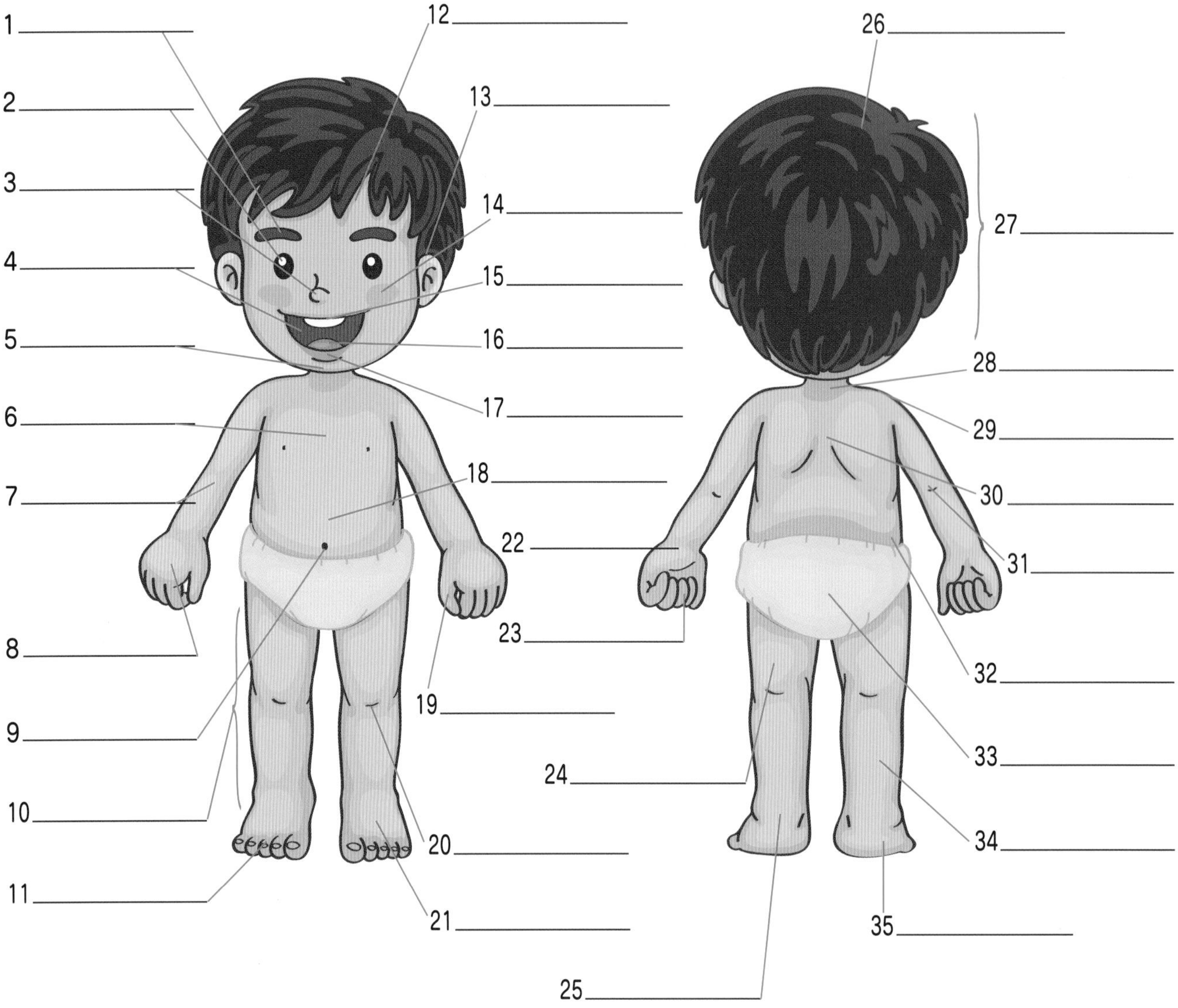

Illustrations on page 21 and 139 by Seina Meadows.

Speaking of People [B-909]
人とつながる英語コミュニケーション

1刷 2020年1月24日
6刷 2023年8月30日

著　者 Peter Vincent ピーター　ビンセント
Naoko Nakazato 中里　菜穂子
Alan Meadows アラン　メドウズ

発行者 南雲一範 Kazunori Nagumo
発行所 株式会社　南雲堂
〒162-0801 東京都新宿区山吹町361
NAN'UN-DO Co., Ltd.
361 Yamabuki-cho, Shinjuku-ku, Tokyo 162-0801, Japan
振替口座: 00160-0-46863
TEL: 03-3268-2311（営業部: 学校関係）
03-3268-2384（営業部: 書店関係）
03-3268-2387（編集部）
FAX: 03-3269-2486
編集者 加藤　敦

装　丁 銀月堂
組　版 Office haru
検　印 省　略
コード ISBN978-4-523-17909-2 C0082

Printed in Japan

E-mail nanundo@post.email.ne.jp
URL https://www.nanun-do.co.jp/